D1648134

Praise for *Selling Without Selling Out*

"Sunny has written an invaluable guide to an extremely important challenge: how to consciously sell a business in such a way that its purpose remains intact and all stakeholders benefit. Too many businesses are started with an exit plan that is all about creating a big payday for the founder but causes undue suffering for the other stakeholders and jeopardizes the company's purpose. I highly recommend this very practical, reliable book from someone who has learned these lessons the hard way."

—Raj Sisodia, co-founder and co-chairman of Conscious Capitalism Inc.

"In this book, Sunny shines a spotlight into the 'black box' of private equity and credibly demystifies the funding or sale of a business. A must-read for any founder or owner who is considering raising capital or liquidity."

—Brian Schultz, CEO of Studio Movie Grill

"Sunny draws an important parallel between environmental sustainability—taking care of the planet—and business ecosystem sustainability. For business owners considering an equity transaction, he provides considered and experienced counsel about decisions, far beyond financial ones, that will enhance all the various stakeholders, help ensure the long-term sustainability of the business, and avoid 'seller's remorse.'"

—Garrett Boone, co-founder and chairman emeritus of The Container Store

"Certifying as a B Corp is a transparent and public commitment to your stakeholders that you will stay true to your mission. In *Selling Without Selling Out*, Sunny gives readers a step-by-step guide to preserving such important commitments throughout and after a sale process."

—Jay Coen Gilbert, co-founder of B Lab

"Sunny's insights allowed me to explore options I never would have considered when selling my business. It shifted my focus from planning the 'wedding day'—the terms of the transaction—to planning the 'marriage'—the best long-term interest of my entire stakeholder community. I believe taking this approach provided the best odds for our culture of care to continue and thrive for years to come."

—Steve Hall, founder of driversselect

"When you've spent years building a business, how you sell it—and who you choose to sell it to—will have a massive impact on your life and the lives of all of your stakeholders. If you care deeply about preserving the unique DNA that led to your business' success and enriching your life and the lives of your stakeholders, this book is a must-read, period."

—Brian Mohr, co-founder of Y Scouts

"Choosing a capital partner or selling your business is one of those fork-in-the-road experiences when it's both most critical and most difficult to champion the principles of conscious capitalism. This books shows you how it's done from those who have been there."

—John Mackey, co-founder and CEO of Whole Foods Market

"Selling your company is one of the single biggest decisions you'll make in your business life, if not the biggest—so it's critical to get it right. Sunny's book is a must-read!'

—Verne Harnish, founder Entrepreneurs' Organization (EO) and author of *Scaling Up (Rockefeller Habits 2.0)*

"Want to sell your business and preserve its culture and values? Read this book and make it a soulful sale."

—Patricia Aburdene, author of *Conscious Money* and *Megatrends 2010: The Rise of Conscious Capitalism*

"After pouring your heart and soul into building your business, the prospect of selling can be daunting. This book masterfully outlines practical concepts and questions that I recommend for anyone considering a sale."

—Kip Tindell, co-founder and chairman of The Container Store

"Only a CEO with personal experience in selling a company could have written this book. Sunny has provided us with a holistic primer for leading through the very challenging and high-stakes process of a company sale. This is must-read material for leaders who are at any point in the process of selling their company."

—Dolf Berle, CEO of Topgolf Entertainment Group

"I could have avoided a lot of heartache if I had read this book in advance of selling my companies. It is not an academic tome, nor is it a guide to maximize the selling price, but rather a massively insightful and helpful guide for getting the most life value for seller, employees, investors, and buyers."

—Ron Peri, founder and chairman of Radixx Solutions

"Sunny provides authentic and engaging leader-to-leader insights from his own and others' hard-won experiences. This book is an essential roadmap for peace of mind long after a sale or transaction."

—Scott Mordell, CEO of YPO (formerly known as Young Presidents Organization)

SELLING

without

SELLING

OUT

SELLING

without

SELLING

OUT

**HOW TO SELL YOUR BUSINESS
WITHOUT SELLING YOUR SOUL**

Sunny Vanderbeck

Conscious Capitalism Press

Conscious Capitalism Press
consciouscapitalism.org/press
Conscious Capitalism Press is an imprint of Conscious Capitalism, Inc.
The Conscious Capitalism Press logo is a trademark of Conscious Capitalism, Inc.

Cover design by Pete Garceau
Text design by Sheila Parr
Cover image © iStockphoto / wragg

Cataloging-in-Publication data is available.
ISBN Hardcover: 978-1-7336327-0-6
ISBN Digital: 978-1-7336327-1-3

Printed in the United States of America
First Edition
10 9 8 7 6 5 4 3 2 1

CONTENTS

YOUR BUSINESS,
YOUR SALE

Nobody understands unless they've been in the chair. They don't know what it means to build something from nothing or to bear the responsibility of sustaining a business that's been in the family for two generations or more. They certainly don't know what it means to be responsible for a thousand people's livelihoods. Nobody sees the long years, where you just barely made it through. They don't see the nights you spent in the office or the strain you felt when it looked like the business would all fall apart.

The company didn't amount to much in the beginning— your bank statements made it look like less than nothing—but you invested countless hours of sweat equity. Emotional equity. Vision equity. The first decade felt like full-time overtime to keep the business above water until finally, in that last stretch, you made the right choices, and you started to pick up some real success. You finally broke through.

Where once there was nothing, now there is something—
something big. As the company grew and your risk paid off,
your equity started to be worth something to other people.
Now there are investors who will pay a lot of money to have
what you have, but it will never mean to them what it means to
you. That very tail end of your journey is all anybody sees. But
you remember.

Now you're thinking about selling your company or taking
on a capital partner, and nearly everything is at stake. It is possible to get to the other side of a sale and land at a place where
all your needs are met and there's a great outcome for everybody. It is also possible to get to the other side and feel as if
twenty years of your life were wasted, even as everyone around
you celebrates. Take it from me—I've been there.

You'll smile and nod and shake their hands and say, "Oh,
thanks, man" as they congratulate you on your new ability to
buy a jet. But if you've sold to the wrong people or for the
wrong reasons, a voice inside will be saying, "I dismantled my
life's work, and I didn't even know I was doing it."

It is possible to get rich and fail utterly in the same stroke.

I sold my business the wrong way, but then I bought it
back and sold it again the right way. I can tell you there's a
world of difference in the feeling it gives you. If I could share
one thing with you, it's that feeling.

If you only care about how much money you make, I won't
try to change your mind or argue with you about it. But this is
not the book for you. There are many sources of advice on how
to get the highest price for your business, and that's the way

the game is set up anyway. Put this book down and go talk to an investment banker.

For the rest of us who *do* care about something besides money, this book will show you how to find a buyer who shares your sense of what matters.

Many people assume that business is different from the rest of life—that it's all about money and economics. They believe business is not, or shouldn't be, personal. Those people have never built anything before. They don't understand that you didn't build the business just to flip it. There are things you care about that have nothing to do with money, and in my view, it's okay to care about those things. When you sell your business, you'll want to sell it to someone who matches your values. That's the right way to go.

For that reason, it's important to bring all of the things you value to this decision. Lots of people are going to try to influence you or give you advice, and they may have some perspective that you can't see, but they have never been where you are right now.

The professional advisors will tell you they know what's best, and they know just how to get it. If you just follow this process, they say, you'll get a good outcome. They're sort of right, except they're often dead wrong. The process is set up to optimize *their* outcome. Often that outcome coincides with yours, but not always. For them, the transaction is the only thing that matters. If you let the process run you, it will focus on two things only: the most money with the highest probability of closing. But for you, closing is the beginning of the next phase, and only you know what's best for the years ahead. This book aims to help you run the process, so that the things that mattered in building your business can matter just as much in selling it.

In the pages that follow, you will encounter what I learned from my biggest failure—selling my business to the wrong people—and how I applied those hard-won lessons when I bought the company back and sold to the right people. We will work through the reasons for selling as well as how to prepare yourself for a sale, even as you're preparing your company. There are many options for selling, which we will also examine: finding a strategic acquirer, going public, waiting, and more. Then there's the "conscious" seller's mindset: understanding how the sale will impact other stakeholders, from family to community, and what it takes to achieve a good outcome for them.

There is more than one kind of buyer, and we will surface the tactics for finding the right match. Every process encounters its share of puzzles, which we will also endeavor to crack: when starting a process, which team members should know about it? How can you use due diligence to build credibility? What does the buyer really look for in a seller? What's the difference between a "fair" deal and a good deal? In the final chapter, we think through the toughest challenge: how to ensure that you've arrived at a good place on the day after the transaction—the most important day of all.

Throughout this book, you will also hear from many CEOs who have been where you are. Some of them had sales that worked out really well, and some of them wish they had done things differently. You will also hear from some advisors—lawyers, investment bankers, and M&A consultants—in their own words. They will all say that the repercussions of the choices you make will hit you on the day after close. On that day, you will be alone with your thoughts, and the tone of those thoughts will depend on whether you were able to be honest with yourself about what's really important.

For some CEOs, the decision to sell their business or take on a capital partner starts with a general unease with the way things are going. You might live for five years with a nagging sense of uncertainty–that the status quo isn't quite working and something has to change. If that's where you are, or if you have finally decided to act, I can help you. What is important to me is that you arrive at a place where you can look back long after your transaction and feel at peace with the decisions you made.

Here's what I don't want for you. I don't want you to have to fake it after you sell your business. I don't want you to have to pretend that everything is awesome while you die inside a little because the people you sold it to tore down your life's work and turned it into the very thing you built your company to compete against. Whether they fired all your family members or dismantled your company—the largest employer in your town—you've heard the horror stories. I want to help you avoid that nightmare.

You had a vision for your company that got you out of bed every morning and made you willing to mortgage your house and spend 12 hours a day winning customers and changing your industry. I don't want you to watch your business become the very thing you promised it would never be. So pull up a chair, and let's have a chat.

This book focuses on the non-monetary aspects of selling your business, but it's not because money isn't important. I don't want you to take a low-ball offer from a buyer, and I don't expect you to be happy with one. What I've learned is that it's okay for money to be important, but that your happiness and satisfaction are likely to be driven by other things.

Everything in a traditional auction process is designed to get you a good price for your business and to feed all of the advisors out of the proceeds. But price is not something to maximize in this instance—it's a threshold.

For many CEOs, their threshold for cash at close is just enough money so they can maintain their current standard of living indefinitely and without worry while giving some away to causes that matter to them.

In other words, money only matters up to a point. If you are only going to make a couple of million dollars from a business that's worth fifty, you've got a money issue. But once you get enough, whatever enough is, the next marginal dollar doesn't add much value. You won't miss it, and it isn't what will make you sad when you look back. If you make the right decision for your company, your head, heart, and wallet will all be happy.

One sure way to put yourself on the path to selling out is to get overly focused on any one dimension of the transaction. Whether it's money in general, cash at close versus rollover, or any other sort of obsession over a single dimension, it's dangerous, because you'll miss the things that matter. Looking at the world through the lens of your banker's spreadsheet makes the world a math problem, not a novel. But if you think about all the defining moments of your life, chances are they weren't about metrics.

Imagine your children are about to leave home. You spent twenty years raising your kids in the way you thought was right, and now you're about to send them off in one direction or another. You'll pass them on to the world, hoping they hold on to that character you instilled and make the right choices for themselves. In your final words to them while they're under your roof, will you tell them to forget who they are and chase the money? Of course not.

When your daughter comes to you and asks how to choose a job, you don't tell her to take the highest-paying option available at any given time and to move to a higher-paying job whenever she can. Most agree that the best advice for her is to take the path that's most fulfilling. When your son asks your advice on whom to marry, you tell him to find someone he loves, enjoys, and feels compatible with, not to marry the first heiress he meets.

There's a lot of good advice out there about how to handle careers and marriage, and even how to advise your children, because most people have careers and marriages and children. But most people have never been a CEO or sold a company, and there isn't as much of a body of knowledge out there for us.

However, what is true for every business owner in this country also holds true for you: It's guaranteed that someday, someone else is going to run your business. Even if it's a family business and you transfer it to the next generation, you will want to ensure that the new owners build on the things that you value. If this sale is an exit for you, then your company is about to leave the safety of your guardianship, and the conversation is no different. You've set it up so that it runs in a way consistent with your values, and it will be disappointing if those values are violated as soon as you turn your back.

The same holds true when you plan to stay on at your company. Sellers often get overly focused on price, which can come back to bite them—even in the money department. There are buyers out there whose strategy is to agree on the asking price but then take back some of that money in details of the contract. So if you pick the highest bidder, be prepared for the letter of the deal, not the spirit of the deal.

There are clues in the way an investment firm presents itself to the world. Does its name mean something? In many cases, it's meaningless. But sometimes it can tell you a lot about what matters to them. Ask the question.

The choices you make about how to sell your business or take on a partner don't disappear once you reach the finish line. They have very significant implications after the deal is done. But if you're like most CEOs, you won't give enough thought to the day after. You just want this thing to happen. It's your ticket, your gold medal, your crowning achievement. You're running to the day when the wire clears. It's closing day, and you're pressing "refresh" on your bank account. Nothing happens all morning, then suddenly the balance grows by a couple of digits. It just happened. The deal is done!

Now what?

OVERVIEW

This is a book about selling your business in a way you can stand behind long after the deal is done. It includes the stories of many entrepreneurs, but it comes from a place of personal experience. I've lived it myself, more than once, and this is the book I wish I had read before I started. There are things nobody talks about, things that matter just as much as, and sometimes more than, money. In this book, I'm going to talk about them. For those of you who think you don't have time to read a full book, I understand. What follows is a short overview of what the book covers. I hope that when you realize that selling your business or taking on an investor is one of the few irrevocable decisions in life, you will choose to read on.

Where I'm Coming From

My way of looking at business is closely tied to "conscious capitalism." Growing up outside taught me that the world works as a network of ecosystems. Everything is connected to everything else. In just the same way, no business is an island. A company exists in an ecosystem of customers, employees, suppliers and the community. Focus on the needs of that ecosystem, and in the long term, it will take care of you.

A long-term view necessarily leads to a conscious strategy, and businesses that focus on short-term profits often burn bridges with their stakeholders. I believe that profit is a trailing measure of the value you create for all of your stakeholders—the people who help your company thrive.

Choosing the right buyer or investor means finding a fit that provides the best overall value for your entire ecosystem, including yourself and your family.

Getting Ready

The process of getting your business ready for sale begins with taking a deep look at some big questions you may never have thought about. Why does your business exist? What are your priorities? What do you care about most, both personally and professionally? These are not trivial questions, and they deserve reflection.

There are lots of reasons you might be thinking of finding an investor or acquirer, but don't forget to take the long view. If you start with the end in mind—what you want the day after closing day to look like—you can keep short-term concerns in perspective.

Perhaps the day-to-day experience of running the business has changed, either because your fun-to-fear ratio has changed, the business has outgrown its systems, or you are simply burnt out from years of continuous stress.

Family businesses go through changes that can lead owners down the road to a sale. Whether the next generation is uninterested or not yet ready to lead, or someone needs to be bought out, an outside investor is sometimes the best solution.

In other cases, the search for an investor or a partner comes from a place of excitement. The business is ready to go to the next level and take on a huge challenge, if only you had the right resources and team.

It will be much easier to focus on what matters if the basics are already in place. Get yourself and your business organized ahead of time and be ready to speak honestly about what is important to you.

Your Options

A clear picture of where you stand right now will also clarify your range of realistic options. Your first option is to do nothing—waiting can be as strategic as selling, if you know why you are doing it—but you will continue to shoulder all of the risk and own all of the downside as long as you retain ownership. Just be careful about falling into what I call the "one-more-year" trap.

You may want to pursue an insider sale or even take your company public, but most companies are looking at two broad categories of buyers or investors. You should know beforehand whether a strategic buyer is best for your business or whether a financial buyer would be a better fit. In a strategic acquisition, a larger company sees value in incorporating your business into its own, bringing your message and your product to many more customers. Just know that your company will change dramatically and so will your job.

A financial investor, such as a family office or private equity fund, values your business for what it is today and what it could be tomorrow. But, traditional financial investors tend to suffer from short-term-itis, collecting companies like baseball cards they can't wait to trade in for cash. I think this is a real problem. Fortunately, a new category, the entrepreneurial investor, is qualified to offer not only long-term capital but also advice and first-hand operating experience to help you take your business to the next level.

Choosing Wisely

Getting to know a buyer takes time—more than an investment banker will want you to spend with them in a traditional auction process. Insist on spending that time, so that you can ask the hard questions about what the buyer is planning to do with your company. Take a trip to their headquarters and see whether the face they show the world matches their real culture. Let any warning signs be a signal to slow down and demand clear answers.

You may want to consider running a limited process, where you select just a few candidates to get to know. Investment bankers and lawyers have their own set of interests, and you cannot rely on them to look out for your long-term happiness. You have hired them for their expertise, so use those strengths to guide you, but be clear about what matters to you. There will be moments when you have to speak up, or be swept away by a cookie-cutter process designed only to close the deal.

Getting It Closed

Hitting or beating the numbers in your projections will carry a lot of weight with an investor. On the other side, red flags pop up when a business relies too heavily on any one element, whether that is its CEO, a key customer, or a major supplier.

The trick is not to get distracted by emotions and irrelevant details in a sale process. A good deal is far more important than a "fair" deal. Before the process begins, write down what you imagine success will look like. Be specific about what you want financially, what you want for each stakeholder, and what you want the next stage of your company to look like. Consider drawing up a "spirit of the deal" document with your buyer to refer back to when things get heated.

The Day After

Once diligence is completed and the wire goes through, life after close begins. The transaction may have been an exit plan for you, in which case your task is to use your newfound freedom to build an identity for yourself that doesn't revolve around your business. But if you stay, you will be dealing firsthand with the consequences of the decisions you made as you sold your business or took on a new investor.

My hope for you is that you will get clear on what is important and see an extraordinary outcome that reflects what matters to you.

CHAPTER ONE

SELLING, BUYING, AND RESELLING MY COMPANY

When I was 23, I started a company with colleagues from Microsoft. Four years in the United States Army Rangers had given me grit. Two years at Microsoft had given me a sense of where things were going in technology. I didn't have the backing of a venture capitalist, but I had a credit card. I was ready to be an entrepreneur.

It was 1996 and we understood that people were going to start using the internet much more intensely for every aspect of business. Large companies and fast-growing smaller companies wanted to sell products on the internet or make contracts and book appointments there, but they didn't have the expertise to keep it all working reliably. We knew we could help.

It was never about the money. It was almost as if once we had the idea for our company, Data Return, we just had to do it. I would wake up every day and see the opportunity in front of me to work on something that had never been done before. Both of my two prior stops—the Rangers and Microsoft—had extraordinary cultures, and it was really important to me that we make Data Return an awesome place to work.

Once we were established, our job was to solve compelling problems for engaging people while building a spot in the market and making a difference. Making a bunch of money was the score, not the game, and it never figured prominently in our thinking. Now, twenty years later, I still get notes from former teammates who tell me how special our workplace was for them and that they've never seen anything like it since.

Our company was in the business of building mission-critical web infrastructure. Whether it was insurance processing or surgical scheduling for every hospital on the island of Manhattan, our job was to keep it running. When people filed their taxes at H&R Block or built their profiles on Match.com and it didn't work, that was on us. Our customers had designed their online application, and they needed to ensure their customers could conduct whatever transaction they were attempting. We didn't write the software, but we kept everything running—the databases, the network, and all the servers.

We had some of the best technology folks in the world at Data Return, and having come from Microsoft, we had seen how a lot of these systems worked. Our business was right on the cutting edge of innovation that would shape our world in the century to come. (In 2005, for example, we built the first cloud computing that was ready for business.)

The thing about working on the cutting edge is you never really know how to do what you're trying to do because nobody else has done it before either. But we knew a little bit more than anybody else because that's where we focused all of our time and energy. We were just early enough in the market that the knowledge base we accumulated through experience, collecting best practices across thousands of environments, was enough to get us far ahead of the competition.

We grew at a crazy pace—40% every quarter. For the first couple of quarters, that's not a big deal, but in the 12th and 13th quarter, you're in sheer liftoff. This continued for more than three years. When I was 27 years old, we took the company public on the Nasdaq.

Then, just 90 days away from profitability, the March 2000 dot-com crash nearly brought down the economy, and everything ground to a halt. Half of our customer base vanished, growth stopped in its tracks, and the whole world seemed to be holding its breath. To keep up with our crazy rate of expansion, we had built our hiring engine around rapid growth. We had to hire at least a quarter ahead of our current size in order to anticipate our future needs. The problem with that necessity is that when growth finally stops—often suddenly—you've already hired at least 40% more staff than you need.

Everyone in our industry had too many people, and employees were well aware of what that meant for them. Over the course of the next year, we had to lay off hundreds of employees. I felt awful about it, and the trauma would stay with me for a long time.

The Sale that Got Away

Once we got our bearings in this new world of scarcity, it was clear to us that we needed to be a bigger company. Our economic model required a minimum size in order to work. In particular, our biggest challenge was in finding customers. We had a very tight lens on who our best customers were, so to find one customer who was a really good fit for us, we had to identify ten potential ones. Once those customers signed on, they loved us, but we spent too much time and energy finding them. It was too hard, it wasn't in flow, and it wasn't working.

We needed either to be part of a larger company or to take on more capital. Taking on more capital would buy us more time to figure things out, but it wouldn't fundamentally change the situation. My concern was that it wasn't clear how long this unprecedented downturn was going to last. It was time to sell the business.

The only sustainable solution would be to sell the business into a strategic acquirer, and the best acquirer was right in front of our noses. Data Return had a close relationship with Compaq, which was a logical buyer in every way. Compaq was an early investor in the company, beginning in the late 1990s. We were also a Compaq customer. We even shared a board member. If we were inside Compaq, our customer-base problem would be solved, because all of Compaq's customers would become our potential customers, and thousands of salespeople would start offering our services.

Under CEO and Chairman Michael Capellas, Compaq was in a phase of strengthening its relationship with Microsoft. As a result of those efforts, it became the key strategic partner for the release of the Windows 2000 operating system, and Data Return had built a market position as the undisputed expert on the Compaq-Microsoft platform. From Compaq's perspective, it made sense to bring our managed hosting business into the company.

Over the years, we got to know Compaq very well, partly because its culture was so collaborative. Compaq's executives noticed that we were buying a lot of their servers and putting them to new uses. Twenty years ago, a big data center with a thousand servers in the same room was a new and crazy-sounding phenomenon, and it came with a host of issues and opportunities.

As a customer, we saw that Compaq's response to being pushed in new ways was to seek out our insights. The president of its server division would pull in all the engineers to meet with us and hear about what was working for us and what kinds of changes would be helpful. In those days, people weren't yet talking about how culture could be a critical competitive advantage. But even then, Compaq had a strong culture of continuous improvement, and it aligned well with ours.

Data Return was a much smaller company, which meant that we could move fast. In building culture as well as setting strategy, we put a premium on speed. We were also a learning organization that invested considerable amounts of time and resources into developing our team.

So when, in the year 2000, Compaq offered to buy Data Return, we knew it was the perfect fit. Not only were our cultures compatible, but all our stakeholders—our customers, our employees, and our suppliers—stood to benefit from the transaction.

A sale to Compaq would have been a real win for our customers, who were struggling to survive the dot-com crash. The aftershocks devastated some of our competitors—billion-dollar companies—so even size didn't ensure stability. Our customers, shaken by the tech sector's volatility, sometimes asked for our financials before they would make a purchase. That was understandable, if unusual. In signing up with us, they were betting that we had the financial wherewithal to endure the crash's fallout and run their most critical business applications.

It would be disastrous for them if we went under, but they had no choice but to take that risk. If they had approached one of the pillars of the industry—an IBM or EDS—those giants would fail at this type of work because they didn't really understand the internet. If they wanted a good result, our customers had to buy service from young, fast companies that had the internet in their DNA.

Under the Compaq umbrella, we would be an island of stability in the midst of utter chaos. We would have the resources to accomplish even more for our customers, and we would create a new spot in the market.

That new-found stability would also benefit Data Return's

employees. As the tech industry continued to bleed jobs, those who hadn't been pink-slipped nevertheless lived with chronic worry that they might not survive the next round of layoffs. A sale to Compaq would allow our employees to take a big, deep breath and enjoy some well-earned stability.

Our employees would find themselves inside the hottest business unit in a very large company, with a lot of opportunities to work on well-funded, innovative projects. All of our leadership was planning on staying, and the acquisition was very important to Compaq's strategy, so the team would remain intact, and career paths would diverge from there according to each employee's interests.

Not only would customers and employees benefit from the transaction, but many of our suppliers would have the opportunity to sell their product to a much larger company, based on their relationship with us. Some of our suppliers, however, would not make the transition to the new business. Given that our acquirer specialized in computers, any of our existing suppliers that sold us computer equipment would lose our business, so the outcome was not uniformly good for all suppliers. Still, our supplier stakeholder group would see an improvement on balance.

I was looking forward to the day after the transaction because my own life was about to get a lot more fun. Ever since we had gone public, I had spent my days with Wall Street guys, dealing with issues related to capital and public company management tasks. I was really excited about going back to an environment where I could spend my day with my team and my customers, working on the fun stuff.

Sign-off day arrived. For almost a year, we had negotiated this deal, homing in on the terms and working out every detail. The final document was to be sent via fax from Compaq CEO Michael Capellas on Friday, August 31, 2001. We were one set of signatures away from a billion-dollar deal.

All day Friday, all I could think about was the closing. I couldn't even pretend to get anything done. Nobody else seemed worried, and everything was meant to be in order, but I was agitated. At 28 years old, I was supposed to be a grownup—with the gravitas that goes with it—but somehow I didn't feel like one. I didn't want to be that guy who calls, asking where the paperwork is, so I forced myself to hold off, but it wasn't easy. The morning passed, and nothing came through on the fax.

I started wondering whether something might be wrong with the fax machine itself. I checked for a paper jam, ran the test fax, worried the line might be tied up and jiggled the back of the machine. The business day came and went, and nothing appeared.

Over the long weekend, I tried to relax. Then on Labor Day Monday, Simon West, our director of marketing, called me at home, which was not his habit. He told me to turn to CNN. The chyron read: <<Hewlett-Packard and Compaq Agree to Merge>>.

Just like that, the deal was off. I didn't need to wait for the next day's somber phone call to know that the $25 billion deal with HP would have to be Compaq's only priority for the next couple of years. Even though we later pointed out to Compaq's executives that under the terms of the merger agreement, they could still go through with the Data Return acquisition, we knew they weren't about to risk introducing any further instability.

Through unforeseeable circumstances completely external to us, our dreams for a future with Compaq were over, and they were never coming back. Over the next six months, we had to pick up the pieces and return to the beginning of what had been a year-long process. The difference this time was that we were now at a much weaker starting point. We were not profitable because our primary objective had been growth and—with the Compaq deal looming—we hadn't been raising capital to lengthen our runway. It wasn't so dire that we only had weeks to work with, but certainly our runway did not extend beyond a year.

The markets in 2001 were still recovering from the burst bubble, our market cap was something like $400 million, and it was very difficult to raise capital. The bitter irony was that prior to the dot-com crash, there was more money available to us than we could spend, and we had turned down large offers of capital. We had also declined the option of making a secondary public offering, to sell 10% of the company for a quarter of a billion dollars in cash. Lacking a use for the proceeds, we determined it would be a bad trade for our shareholders.

I can only imagine what it would have been like to have had a quarter of a billion dollars of cash at our disposal after the dot-com implosion, when the whole world seemed to be enduring a fire sale. Companies that had a hundred million dollars in cash were trading with a market cap of less than a hundred million. Anyone with that much capital could have gone on a mergers and acquisitions spree and built a juggernaut of a business. But we had said no to it, and I chalked that up under lessons thoroughly learned. Some lessons have to be experienced to really sink in, and it's particularly difficult to learn the lesson that even though things feel like they will continue forever, the world can change dramatically in the blink of an eye.

Selling to the Wrong Guys

We found ourselves returning to the same faces we had met the year before. "Oh, you're back." The only action that seemed to make sense was to sell the company as part of a strategic acquisition, but the other similarly-sized companies in our line of business were struggling, too. We began a formal process to try to reel in a much bigger fish.

Then one day I was speaking at a conference, and an investment banker approached me. He said he knew we were running a process, and he had an idea for me—would we consider Divine, a technology consulting and software company. This looked like a reasonable fit because Divine shared with Compaq the ability to solve our customer problem.

From Divine's perspective, with the bursting of the dot-com bubble it was safer to buy established companies than to invest in startups, and we had demonstrated an ability to help companies use the internet to communicate with customers and suppliers. Divine delivered a billion in revenue, so from our perspective, the business was big enough to provide lots of potential customers. Its strategy was to buy a number of tech companies and integrate all of our products into one "suite" to create an extended enterprise. The network of products would help corporations exploit the expanding promise of the internet. That story appealed to us. We accepted Divine's offer.

Despite the near-miss with Compaq, this would be the first time I actually sold my company. Just as parents talk about the outsized grief they feel when their first child goes off to college, I had a strong emotional reaction to the reality that I had poured my life into the business—and now it was time to let go. Despite all the good reasons for selling the company, it all comes crashing down when you realize you've actually done it. In fact, my response was physiological. When we announced the transaction, I had a 102-degree fever. As it turned out, my body already sensed what my head couldn't yet conceive: this deal wouldn't end well.

Within 90 days of the sale, it became clear that Divine's strategy and its execution were wholly disconnected. It was going to have the same problem Data Return had had: landing the right customers. But whereas we had done everything in our power to fix that problem, our acquirer wasn't as open to change.

I realized that we had been so impressed with the senior management team's track record and the overall story of how we might fit into an expanded enterprise, we had neglected to do the deeper reverse diligence and get to know this company from the bottom up. With Compaq, we hadn't had to do much reverse diligence because we had all the important information already.

Whereas in theory, the consulting team handed leads to the sales team, that wasn't really happening. We might have known that, and many other problems, if we had just called up a handful of CEOs out of the 40 companies they had acquired. Instead, we spent about half a day having Divine's executives talk through their plan on a surface level.

Even though they were rock stars, the management team was the product of another age. Divine was running old playbooks on new realities in a different business, and it wasn't working.

So I did what I was used to doing as an entrepreneur, and what I later discovered makes me a less than ideal employee in a corporate environment. I took ownership of the problem and acted. There were 17 business unit heads or functional heads in the company, and I got them all together in a room and laid out the situation as I saw it. I made a pretty convincing case for change.

Even though the cash situation was not dire yet, I tried to inject some urgency by asserting that we had 100 days to make the company profitable. If we couldn't make the deadline we set for ourselves, we weren't going to get it done in a year, either, and at the end of that year, we would be in a bad place. Then I went around the room, asking each unit head individually, "Are you in?" I wanted full, unequivocal, hands-down buy-in, and I got it from all but one person. That person also said yes, but with some equivocation.

I gathered my 16 ½ votes and took it to the CEO. I told him everything I had told the business unit heads, and I shared my projections about the short time frame for turning things around. The whole company is already on board, I said, and all you have to do is say yes. He said no.

Looking back, I can see how extraordinarily threatening it must have been for him. Nobody wants to hear that the strategy is flawed and the execution is a mess. Coming in with the team's consensus, it must have seemed as if I were just about staging a coup. But that's not how I saw it—in my way of thinking, I couldn't see the company failing and shrug it off as somebody else's problem.

In February of 2003, a year after that 'no' from the CEO, our acquirer filed for a Chapter 11 bankruptcy.

Buying Back My Own Company

Divine had taken stakes in almost 80 technology companies before filing for bankruptcy. Some, like a library subscription service it had purchased in 2001, were in dire straits, but many of the companies were still in reasonable shape. In 2003, a 26-hour auction was held in Boston to sell off pieces of the business. My company was one of those pieces being sold, and I wanted it back.

The only problem was, I had been barred from directly bidding. I had to try to get it back indirectly, partnering with an existing bidder.

If a competitor bought it, I knew Data Return would be dismantled and I wouldn't have a job—basically my worst nightmare. I wanted us to have a fresh start, but I had to stand by and wait for the news that would determine my future. Guess how much sleep I got that night . . .

Fortunately, we ended up with a few low-ball competitor bids looking to salvage a few contracts, and we were able to buy our company back for less than a third of the price our buyer had paid us for it. We retained 100 members of Data Return's original team and hired 40 more in sales and marketing to re-establish our presence in the market.

Buying Data Return back gave us a chance to reset a number of things. For one, we no longer had the strain of running as a public company. We were private again, and I was much happier in that environment. It took about a year of intensive work to let people know we were back and to get the company running the way we wanted. Our company's next phase would look quite different, partly because the market had changed. With a better balance between profitability and growth, we emerged from our misadventures with a much better business than it was before.

Selling to the Right Guys

Our eventual acquirer, Terremark, sold products that were not directly in competition with ours but offered a third option to solve the same web infrastructure problem. It was a do-it-yourself package that gave the customer a connection to the network and a space in the data center, but with no service to speak of.

By the time we sold Data Return a second time in 2007, I had learned enough to do it right.

Terremark was a company that caught my interest, but our investment bankers' resistance. Their advice was to skip it—they didn't believe Terremark was a real buyer and thought it was a waste of time to include them in the process. I remember every detail, down to where I was standing, when I insisted that we put them on the shortlist of prospects. The moment is anchored in my mind because it defined so many things that happened later, and it reinforced the notion that there are decisions only a CEO can make.

Terremark came in with the second-highest bid, but it was clear the company was a great match for us. Partnering with Terremark was the culmination of the new strategy we had adopted in the second incarnation of Data Return. It's hard to overstate the effect of combining those two companies—Terremark's stripped-down offerings and our medium-range and top-of-the-line products—which freed the sales team to sell exactly what customers wanted. Full service? Great idea! Co-location? No problem! The growth rate of the combined business skyrocketed.

The customers saw an immediate benefit, and most of our management team did, too. Though a couple of our leaders were not a fit and did not transition to the new company, many were promoted shortly after the deal. Our VP of Sales became the global VP of Sales for the combined business. Our CMO became the CMO for the whole business, and so on. Personally, I knew from recent experience at Divine that I had too much of an entrepreneurial mindset to fit comfortably in any position other than CEO. When we found Terremark, it was a great outcome for all of the stakeholders, but the corporate environment also meant that for the good of the team—and my own sanity—I had to step away.

When CEOs say they would like to sell 100% but are happy to stay around for a year or two, they really don't want to stay around for a year or two—they want to go right now. I know this because that's how I felt when we sold to Terremark. I would have been okay with helping out in the transition, but I much preferred to leave. In the end, they told me they were ready to take over long before my contractual transition period was up. Part of me was grateful, and part of me found it jarring to suddenly not be needed. But I knew it was time to go.

That last day in the office was surreal. I put everything I had into that business for a decade—I had started it, sweated over it, bled over it, and cried over it. And this was my last day. I believed it was going to be a great fit for everybody, so I wasn't sad but didn't quite know how to feel. I was just not equipped for that day, and nobody around me could help me. What do you say to people on your last day?

I had to have conversations with people, but I hadn't prepared anything to say, and it felt awkward. I could say simply thank you and goodbye, but that didn't feel like enough.

Overall, though, I was happy to be a casualty of that transaction. Stepping back, it was a great feeling to leave my team in good hands, and by that time I was excited about an idea I had been developing for a couple of years with one of our customers, Randy Eisenman. The concept we were building would become Satori Capital, a new kind of private equity firm that we run together to this day.

TAKEAWAYS

Nothing happens until money changes hands. There is little doubt that Data Return would have made a seamless fit with Compaq. From every perspective—including Compaq's—the logic for the sale was unassailable. Then HP emerged, and our future quickly capsized. The lesson I took from the sale that sailed away is that money isn't everything, but it is the start of everything. A game-changing strategy, a high-potential idea, or in our case, a chance to get big fast—no matter how promising, none of that is real until the wire clears. Good leaders live by the well-worn maxim, "The buck stops here." For entrepreneurs and company builders, the buck is where things start.

There's a price to pay when you sell the business: you're no longer in control. We tend to think that making money, winning resources, and gaining throw-weight through a strategic sale is a good thing, which of course it is. However, there's an eye-opening reality for founders who take on investors or who remain with the company after the sale: they no longer have total ownership of their dream. Because Divine's CEO had more control over the company than I did, I worked for him, regardless of my deep connection to the enterprise that I had founded or my natural instinct to act quickly when a problem arose. True, the benefits of taking on an investor or selling to a strategic acquirer can outweigh the cost of potentially losing the ability to execute your vision on your terms. But the lesson remains: Before you take the money, understand that you're going to give up at least some control.

If you've built a company that others want to buy, you have an instinct for what works. Trust it. Because Terremark hadn't done much M&A, our bankers concluded it wasn't a credible buyer and resisted putting the company on our shortlist of potential acquirers. I disagreed. I thought Terremark would make a good strategic fit, so I drew a line in the sand and insisted on adding it to the list. Pushing back wasn't easy. I wasn't clairvoyant. I certainly didn't know that Terremark would turn out to be our buyer. What's more, the bankers are the experts, and it's always wise to listen and reflect on what they say. However, there are moments in the selling process when you've got to rely on your judgment and make the call that only a CEO can make. Bankers are advisors. It is you, the seller, who is ultimately the decider.

CHAPTER TWO

PREPARING A SALE STARTS WITH PREPARING YOURSELF

All CEOs have moments where nothing goes right, and it's not clear whether it will ever get better. The world is collapsing around you and you just don't know how you'll get through the day. But now you have to walk into the final interview with a candidate you really want to hire and tell her how great it's going to be to work for you. You've got to close the sale. Go.

One of a CEO's essential skills is what my wife and I call "TV face," after the time I had to use it on CNBC, in a live, national broadcast. Your mood sets the tone for all of the people around you, and they look to you for reassurance. Especially for employees, the CEO is the champion of hope. No matter what's going on inside you, it's show time. You've got to push down your inner angst, slap on a smile, and go.

Everyone's internal state ebbs and flows, and most people get to express that on the outside to some degree, but not you. Your external state needs to be far steadier, so there's always some tension between that TV face and what's going on underneath it. CEOs don't get sick days, because one day missed means eight meetings cancelled—meetings in which the CEO is a key player, if not the leading figure.

By the time entrepreneurs are deciding whether and how to sell a company, they're already so good at TV face that they can fool even themselves. That's when the skill becomes dangerous. This is not a time to put a happy veneer on things. It's a time to look hard at your own life and be honest about what you need.

The process of getting your company ready for sale actually starts with getting you ready. It begins with a long, deep look at the big questions.

Why does your business exist? Think back to when you started your company and ask yourself why you did it. What drives you to get out of bed in the morning, and what is your company's non-financial reason for being? If your company has a written set of values or a formalized mission or purpose, the beginning of your journey starts there, with why it existed in the first place. Think about what sort of sale might damage the company's ability to carry out that purpose. Consider what sort of transaction will preserve and promote the company's calling. The answers to those questions will form the foundation for what comes next.

What are your priorities? Honestly reckon with why you are pursuing a transaction. If you want money now, you will need to take a different approach than if you are willing to wait for more money later. If your business disappeared tomorrow, who would care? The answer is stakeholders—your employees, your customers, your suppliers, and your community. Imagine what a great outcome would look like for each of them.

Oftentimes as leaders, we place the needs of the business and its stakeholders over the needs of ourselves and our immediate families. This is a time to stop ignoring or forgetting your own needs and to recognize that you and your family are stakeholders, too. Reflect on what a great outcome looks like for you, personally, and for your closest loved ones.

If you don't write it down, it isn't real, so spend some quiet time putting pen to paper and thinking about these additional questions:

- How are you feeling about work?
- What do you want (for yourself and for your company)?
- Are you looking for an exit or do you want to take some risk off the table?
- Do you want to grow faster or larger?
- Is there an opportunity for your business to take off, if only you had the capital or the right team behind you?
- What do you value?
- What does success look like?
- What will be your legacy?
- How important is it for you to be in charge?

Use the worksheets available on SunnyVanderbeck.com to help you get clear on where you are now, and where you want to land in the future.

Reasons to Sell

People sell their business in all kinds of situations, and you need to understand your own very clearly. You may have the option now to retire, but if you feel like you have a lot left to give to your business, you also have the option to find a partner who can help you achieve your vision. Every situation is unique, but the reasons for selling tend to fall into a few broad categories. Here are some of the more common scenarios and what they suggest for the kind of sale that's right for you.

You Aren't Driving the Company, You're Stewarding It

One of the reasons to take on a capital partner is that your appetite for risk is waning. Because you were hungry and put everything into it, you built a great company. For a long time, the business was next to nothing. Then one day you woke up and it was something substantial. Now the company is finally working the way you dreamed it would, and life is good. You take home $5 million a year, and all you have to do to keep the good life is avoid screwing it up. You have become a steward of the company, not its CEO.

The danger in a stewardship mentality is that you stop

doing the very things that got you here. As the business grows, the decisions that cross your desk grow, too. Even if you were comfortable making $500,000 decisions ten years ago, you might have trouble with a $5 million decision today. If it costs you a year and a half's earnings to open a new plant, it might be strategically obvious to do that, but it's much harder now to make that investment.

You're trying hard not to break what you've built, but if you don't take those risks you're breaking it anyway—just more slowly. As the pace of change continues to accelerate, competitive advantage is eroding more rapidly—and more and more companies are finding themselves on the wrong side of the change curve. A company that isn't taking risks or innovating doesn't last long.

I have a lot of empathy for a CEO who finds himself in the stewardship trap, and it's very rewarding to help free somebody from that trap when we build a partnership.

In our first meetings with one potential portfolio company, it was clear that the CEO was facing this problem. He took me through the company's digital marketing results, and it emerged that for every dollar he spent on advertising, that dollar returned in profit within 90 days. Within six months, the advertising paid for itself three times over.

A hungry CEO starting out in his business would respond to that finding very differently than the steward CEO. He would pounce on anything that seemed to be working and do more of it. If he wasn't sure about the data, he would re-allocate resources to resolve any doubts. As soon as he confirmed the ads were working, he would put everything he could into marketing. Sell the furniture. Sell everything not nailed down. You might have nowhere to sit, but you can buy better chairs when it works.

Five years ago, this same CEO would have made some aggressive moves to pursue the opportunity, but something had happened during those five years—and not just the growth of his business. Five years ago, his granddaughter was born with special needs. She would never be able to work, she would require a lot of support throughout her life, so she needed to be in a position where she would never have to worry about money. Her future security had become the most important driver of his business decisions.

Taking on a capital partner was a promising option for him. With the money he took out of the transaction, he could secure the little girl's future and then step back into the business and take on some risk. The old fears of jeopardizing his granddaughter's basic needs would be gone, and he could come back ready to push.

You're Tired

Even when it's working well, running a business imposes an extraordinary amount of stress. Everything is at stake every day, and in many businesses, the CEO has to be on top of every decision. If you've been doing this for 10 or 20 years—much of it spent in fight-or-flight mode—you may be really worn out. Whatever comes next for your business, the next stage for you, personally, has to involve a lot less work. You may also feel as if you need to have all of the ambiguity, risk, and uncertainty lifted from your shoulders. You have been carrying that burden for too long.

Exhaustion is a common reason to sell, and it's something to be honest about, because it does change your choices. If you take on a private equity partner when you are bone tired, you may not have to leave, but you might have to assume a chair-person role, to give yourself some relief from that 70-hour-a-week schedule. If you fool yourself into thinking you can keep up with that same gruelling work routine and then you find your heart isn't in it, you will have a conflict with your buyer. Your new investor will show up fresh and ready to go on Day One, and the pace will accelerate.

Your Children Don't Want the Family Business

Succession in a family business can be tough to get right. You may wake up one day and realize that the work doesn't light up your kids. It's just not who they are. Even though your plan was to pass the business to them, they have no real interest in taking it. It's no favor to hand them a burden, even if it comes as an inheritance.

If the situation really is that they don't want it, choosing the right buyer, whether financial or strategic, will help ensure that your legacy lives on. You won't have the opportunity to be proud of what your kids did with the business, but you can still choose a buyer whose actions might give you that same sense of pride.

Your Children Aren't Ready for the Family Business

Sometimes the timing just isn't right. You're going to be ready to leave before your children or grandchildren will be ready to run the company. The time horizon will not always cooperate. This can be a good time to look for a financial buyer if the culture fit is right. The right financial buyer can put the right systems in place if your kids aren't ready. Taking some chips off the table might also allow you to let go of the business when you do pass on the CEO role to another family member. If you don't have as much at stake, you can let the younger generation make their own mistakes without risking your retirement.

Your Fun-to-Fear Ratio has Changed

A CEO's brain is always consumed with the business, whether things are going well or badly. There is no such thing as work-life balance for most entrepreneurs. It's unlikely that you could build anything of significance on a 40-hour week. When people tell you that you need more balance in your life, they don't understand that's just not how it works. Quality of life for you is not about spending more clock time outside the office—your mind will be on your work anyway—it's about your level of engagement and enjoyment.

If you used to be interested and excited by your work, and now you drag yourself to the office and dread the day, that's useful information. If you spend more time feeling fear than joy, if it's just a lot less fun to be there than it used to be, or if you're frankly bored by the whole thing, that's a real reason to make a change.

The Business has Outgrown Itself

A good reason to look for a partner-style investor is that you just need someone you can entrust with helping to organize your company's systems and processes to fit its new scale, so you don't have to put out fires all day long. Founders don't make good administrators. They feel their way into business. When things take off, they often find the company outgrows their skillsets and outpaces the tools for running it. Entrepreneurial businesses that aren't operationally agile stay small.

We all start our careers with large gaps in our knowledge base, and we teach ourselves and learn from others as we go, but there comes a point where we need to install some solid systems to support day-to-day operations. When I met Britt Peterson, this was the problem he was solving at his company, Longhorn Health Solutions.

Peterson got his start when his dad handed him some business cards and told him to go out and start calling on people. The family business handled wholesale medical supplies and sold them to local doctor's offices, hospitals, and hospice agencies—everything from Band-Aids to examination gloves to adult diapers. By high school, Peterson was working at the warehouse; he moved into sales during college.

Over time, he developed a niche providing Medicaid-covered supplies, which allowed him to bill a government payer directly instead of the individual recipients. He took orders and delivered the supplies all across Texas. As the business grew, he hired his friends, none of whom had any training, and they figured everything out as they went along. It was a lot of fun, there was a lot of laughter and camaraderie, but it got to the point where Peterson's role was overwhelming.

He did payroll for the whole company—about a hundred employees—and he spent a lot of time putting out fires. If his young delivery van drivers were caught breaking rules, or the people in the office got into a petty argument, he had to sort it out. There was no CFO, no HR staff; it was all on Peterson to juggle, and the higher-order CEO tasks, like thinking seriously about strategy, were put aside for another day, another month, some other year. "It got to a point where the things that got us to where we were weren't going to keep working," says Peterson.

Having started the company at 22 years old, with his only training growing up in a small business, Peterson found himself reinventing the wheel when it came to hiring practices, time off, and overtime pay. He wanted to expand the company, but there was no real plan for making that happen.

Peterson had been entering accounting information into QuickBooks, but he needed help putting together more robust information to get a better look at how the business was actually doing. He needed some expert logistics help in shipping supplies to patients, including the negotiations with shippers and manufacturers. Most of all he wanted some help in setting his company's direction. He started looking for a financial partner and found my firm, Satori. Peterson's learning mindset and his openness to collaborating were a great fit for us. We made an investment, rolled up our sleeves together and started to work on the business.

"My job is much more fun than it used to be," says Peterson. "I'm now just responsible for thinking about real big deals and having an unbelievable relationship with the heads of these health insurance companies."

Peterson can be confident all the necessary elements are in place, and he is free to spend time on the things he loves.

You Fear for Your Company's Future

A CEO who doubts the future of his business—or the viability of his industry in the coming years—might feel like he's in a tough spot. Maybe he has a report from Gartner Research that projects four percent growth in his industry over the next ten years, but he sees warning signs signalling a contraction. His apprehension leads him to seriously consider selling—is it wrong for him to present his company in the best possible light if he worries an acquirer is going to have a bad outcome?

It's a complicated question, and it depends on whether the gloomy outlook is based on the CEO's subjective opinion or important information that he should share. A homeowner would do well to put a fresh coat of paint on the walls and de-clutter the living room before putting the house up for sale. The owner might take photos of the building on the sunniest day of the year, from an angle that makes it appear especially spacious. What the owner shouldn't do is put a rug over the gaping hole in the floor and move a bookcase to hide evidence of water damage.

Some entrepreneurs feel as if their business is about to get caught out by the future, but when they really analyze it, they find they're just burnt out and anxious about what comes next. They project their personal feelings onto the whole industry, when the facts might not bear out their fears. On the other hand, they got to where they are because they have the ability to see things others can't, so perhaps they have an insight those industry pundits are missing.

Either way, your company's future depends not on how successful you would be if you continued to own it, but on the strengths, weaknesses, and resources of the buyer. What the business is worth to you may be very different from what it's worth to the acquirer. Strategic buyers will have their own reasons for acquiring a smaller company, and it might not matter to them that you think your boat is sinking. They will arrive with their own set of beliefs about the future of your industry, and your misgivings won't matter.

In a global economy, bigger businesses have all kinds of advantages, so a strategic buyer might be able to do more with your business on the strength of the buyer's access to cheaper money, customers, lobbying power, or better pricing from suppliers. A financial buyer may not have those economies of scale, so if you think the future of your company is less than great, a sale to private equity will not end as well, especially if you are staying.

You Need to Buy Out a Shareholder

As a company grows, its shareholder makeup can become unwieldy. That year when you were fresh out of Christmas gift ideas and you handed out a bunch of tiny slices of equity? Those fourteen cousins who all have a piece of the business, but only half of them work in it? A lot of internal problems can arise from competing interests when some shareholders just want their check while those who work in the business want to put resources into growth.

The differences between owners can be as simple as a mismatch between two business partners' horizons. If the partnership is 50/50, you can become completely stuck. Whose needs come first? A values disagreement between partners can make things even worse, because the trust required for compromise is suddenly missing. Someone needs to be bought out.

Selling can be a solution for everyone, but the form of the sale matters. If you sell to private equity without any rollover (continued investment of your own money in the company), that would be overkill. You fixed the issue for the people who want to go, and you simplified the shareholder base, but now you no longer own the business. Similarly, selling to a strategic buyer is not the right move in this case, because it's too blunt an instrument. Then the company effectively doesn't exist in its current form.

Going public is an option if you have the kind of scale it requires, and that will also give the non-active shareholders liquidity. It can also help you if you have taken on too much debt. But at a smaller scale, your best bet for fixing a shareholder conflict is to sell to a well-aligned private equity firm with a large rollover. You exchange a gaggle of shareholders for a partner who shares your ambitions for growth. Selling part of your company to financial investors means the owners that had been holding the business back have gone happily on their way without you having sacrificed your stake. And if you choose well, those same investors can help you go faster.

You See an Opportunity You Can't Seize Alone

If you don't have the size to take advantage of an opportunity in the market, a merger of equals can be your fast track to scale. However, a merger of unequals can make it all come crashing down. Kevin Fallon experienced both.

Fallon, who ran a small business that specialized in systems integration, successfully used a merger to scale. His business, All-Control Systems (ACS), automated food, chemical, and pharmaceutical manufacturing for Fortune 1000 companies. After 15 years in the industry, Fallon began talking with some of his competitors around the country, and they cooked up a plan to build a national platform by merging five companies. Most of the companies were around the same size, pulling in $10 million or $12 million in sales, but together they could build a national organization that would serve multinational clients.

It was an audacious plan. Fallon moved to Denver, where the new CEO and his company were based, and he began to meld the companies under the banner of TAVA, a small-cap public company listed on the Nasdaq. From an initial sum total of 250 employees, TAVA more than doubled to 600 employees over the next 30 months and grew to include 14 offices across the United States.

"You talk about selling without selling out, well this was definitely that," says Fallon. "We had an alignment of goals, and we were all like-minded. Looking back, it was an incredible thing we were attempting to pull off."

Things really got rolling over the following year, and TAVA was on track to become an established national brand. Fallon kicked up a new business within the company called TAVA Y2K1, which addressed companies' worries over software bugs that might cause chaos once computer calendars marked the new millennium on January 1, 2000. Companies like Pfizer and Coca-Cola were coming to him initially for Y2K fixes, but they would end up bringing TAVA in to deliver remediation services to all of their facilities.

Those outsized opportunities pushed Fallon to build a national sales force. He pulled all of the sales staff out of the regional operations and brought them together in Florida for training, so that any one salesperson could then sell the services of any one of the new company's 14 offices. The real power of the merger hit home as each of the 14 offices shared its strengths. It quickly became clear that in this merger, two plus two equaled six.

Now they could go after the Fortune 500 companies, offering them a suite of services broader than any other independent company—so broad that they could make the leap to consolidate all of their local systems integration vendors into just one national vendor.

It was with a feeling of invincibility that they took a meeting with Real Software, a large public company on the Belgian stock exchange and one of the top 20 companies in the Belgian market, to explore a sale. It was 1999, just before the technology bubble would burst, and there were acquisitions, expansion, and money flying everywhere.

"The venture capital world was off the Richter scale in stupidity at the time. They were putting valuations on companies with nothing," remembers Fallon. "Real Software, in particular, had real swagger."

The Belgian company had technology businesses all over—not just in Belgium but in France, Ireland, England, and Germany. It wanted to repurpose those products for the North American market, and TAVA seemed like just the platform to bring Real Software to a new continent. After a six-month negotiation, the TAVA team accepted an offer. TAVA sold the company for $8 per share, 30 months after the founders had formed it at $1.30 per share. It was a great outcome, financially speaking, for the investors, and it came to a total price of $200 million.

Fallon had hopes that TAVA might expand into Europe through the sale and benefit from some of the technologies owned by its acquirer. For example, the buyer owned a maintenance management system in Belgium that Fallon thought he could use in the United States. There was a hidden problem with that idea, though—the software was originally written in Flemish. Though the business-focused employees in Belgium spoke both English and Flemish, most of the people in maintenance primarily spoke Flemish. That issue would come to show that all the seeming synergies would be one-way benefits for the Belgian company.

The CEO of Real Software owned 10 percent of the business, which made him a billionaire, and when he made decisions, he did so with force and confidence. Fallon was skiing with his family in Colorado when he got the call from Aartselaar, Belgium. Real Software's management had been thinking about what they wanted to do with their new American acquisition, and they had decided to have all of the salespeople report directly back to the operations of each of the local facilities. The Belgians didn't like this national sales model.

"It totally ripped the carpet out from under us," recalls Fallon. "I said, 'You just paid $200 million for us, and you may as well shoot that $200 million in the head because you're going to blow up the whole company if you do this.'" He wrote up a letter of resignation so that he wouldn't have to watch his work fall to pieces. Sure enough, the strategy failed. With its selling machine fractured, TAVA became nothing more than a collection of 14 offices. Now, it is no more.

When Fallon first sold his business in 1996, his aim was to build the company into something greater than it could ever have become on its own. For a brief, shining moment, he saw that dream come to fruition, but when the new company sold again a couple of years later, it all came crashing down. The particulars of his story clearly show that money is sometimes the least important aspect of a sale— Fallon found happiness with a change of ownership that held very little immediate financial benefit, and then he sold the company for hundreds of millions and came to regret it. Fallon may be an extreme example, but versions of it play out all the time in the M&A world. We'll revisit Fallon later in the book, as he continues to accrue lessons from sale transactions.

For now, it makes sense to quickly rewind the reasons to sell: You're stewarding the company instead of driving it. You're tired. Your children don't want the business or aren't ready for it. You're not having as much fun. You've outgrown your systems. You fear the future. You need to buy out a shareholder. You need partners to scale. Doubtless there are others, but these are the most common scenarios for selling a business. One or more might apply to you. When you reflect deeply on why you want to sell and define the logic for it, you're better prepared for the next step, which is to find a buyer who best meets your needs.

To Make a Match, Define Your Values

Knowing your own position and priorities can make finding a partner much more straightforward. One of our Satori portfolio companies, Gibraltar Business Capital, has a 65-year history of lending money to small businesses to help them go through a transition. Scott Winicour's father acquired the company in 1991, and when he was ready to retire, Scott bought him out in partnership with a family office. The business had started to expand more rapidly. Gibraltar's inventory was cash, and to grow it, Scott needed more investors.

Winicour wanted to find a buyer with a good culture fit. To

do that, he first had to understand and articulate his own company's culture. "When I think of culture, I'm trying to build a business that has the feeling of a family," he says. "We spend 40 hours a week, sometimes more, in our office working with one another and with the various stakeholders. That's more time than you spend with your true family."

The company had articulated three values that it uses in the hiring process, to make sure employees are a good cultural fit. Every quarter, there is a small reward for an employee who has excelled at living up to the company's core values. Each defined value applies to Gibraltar's day-to-day business activities:

Authentic: We stand up for what we believe and we openly share our point of view. We respect when others do the same. We can win as a team by fostering open communication with all of our stakeholders.

Reliable: We are dependable not only for the source of capital we provide but also for how we carefully manage the relationships we develop. Consistency is key to building trust.

Thoughtful: We recognize that every decision impacts someone. We place ourselves in the position of our stakeholders so that we can present comprehensive, efficient solutions while still being mindful of acceptable levels of risk.

Given the clarity of those values, the starting place was for Gibraltar to find an investor who was authentic, reliable, and thoughtful. Winicour also knew that Gibraltar was entering a growth phase. He couldn't go through the distraction of raising capital again in five years. He wanted someone who could hold onto the business for 20 years.

Winicour ended up choosing Satori as an investor because his conversations with us embodied the values of authenticity and thoughtfulness. Here's how, in his own words:

> The Satori guys don't really give advice—they talk a lot about shared experiences. No one at Satori has ever said, "You're doing this." They say things like, "Hey, have you thought about this? Here's a suggestion." They talk about when they were in the same position with the same problem, as well as how they handled it, and how it turned out. For me, it's helpful to know what worked for someone in my shoes, so that I can decide whether to apply the same solution.
>
> The investor-founder relationship is no different than any other relationship. Whether it's a husband and wife, a parent and child, or an employee and employer, it's all about building trust. Satori didn't just hand us a bunch of millions of dollars. They said they were going to invest in us because they thought we had the right strategy and the right platform—and that we were the right people. What they meant by that last piece is that we were open to listening to what they have to offer. I find that a really interesting approach to developing relationships. As a result, Gibraltar is now hitting a critical scale I always hoped we could reach.

When you have a secure sense of what's important to you, finding the right match in an investor can feel like looking in a mirror. The more work you do up front in defining your wants and needs, the less energy you will have to misdirect toward buyers who were never right for your business.

In the next chapter, with your reason to sell clearly in mind, we will talk about your options.

TAKEAWAYS

Take a hard look within. As an entrepreneur, you have to articulate a future for stakeholders that doesn't yet exist and that you might not fully believe in—at least not yet. However, that skillset won't serve you well when the time comes to sell. In fact, the first step to *selling out* starts when you're not honest about where you're at and you don't define what you want. To avoid that trap, recall that your own particular way of seeing and making sense of the world helped you build a successful business. Now it's time to shift that singular perspective from the world to yourself. Cast a cold, objective eye on where you really are, what you really think, and what you really want.

Before you think about your enterprise's value, get clear on what you value. The bankers never talk about the day after the sale, because they all leave and move on to the next deal, while you are left with the consequences of your decisions. You will feel a lot better about the outcome if you look beyond the money and do the hard work of deeply understanding the other things you care about: Your legacy? Your stakeholders? Achieving bigger business goals? Retaining ownership? Check your answers with your forum—that is, your informal board of advisors. The people who know you best will help you cut through the fog and identify what matters most. For me, some of the most valuable input has come through my involvement with Young Presidents Organization (YPO) and through the Stagen Leadership Program. I would recommend those networks to any CEO who wants to build their forum.

CHAPTER THREE

YOUR OPTIONS
FOR SELLING

Now that you are clear about your priorities and values, your range of options will emerge from that reality. You are faced with a set of alternatives that differ from each other in important ways. Keep the truth of your situation firmly in mind as you explore those possibilities. Others have knowledge you need, but only you know what is truly important.

People who have a financial incentive in seeing you sell will have a narrow perspective on your range of options. Taking on a minority investor or doing a debt recapitalization might be deemphasized to you because those options do not result in advisors receiving much money. If your banker sees you as a candidate for a public offering and they offer services in that area, you may see them pushing hard for that. But just because you have an option available, that doesn't mean you should take it. An option is a tool to accomplish a specific set of objectives.

In a formal sales process, an investment banker may send the pitch book for your business to hundreds of potential buyers, including corporate acquirers, private equity firms, and family offices. The intent is to maximize your possible buyers and provide a menu of offers and terms. Having decided to sell, you now have multiple pathways for finding the right buyer. With few exceptions, though, you should go into the process having already decided on the path you want to take. Based on my experience, there are eight common options to choose from.

1) Do Nothing

You are under no obligation to sell, even if you are feeling some of the stressors that can induce people to go down that route. Maybe the fatigue you are facing is temporary, and maybe it doesn't rise to the level that would cause you to act. Maybe selling looks too much like an easy way out of a business challenge, and you would like to fight through this one alone if you can. Waiting can be as strategic as selling, if you know why you are waiting.

For example, if your real objective is to build a billion-dollar-plus business, and that's your life's work, you will have to decide again and again *not* to sell. It may take forty years of fighting through downturns to build another Apple, but there is some slim chance you can get there. If that's your mission, don't get distracted by the people who want to buy your growing enterprise—just don't forget how much you are risking. The only way to make a billion dollars is to be irrationally, unreasonably optimistic and never sell. Then again, that same behavior pattern is the one that might leave you broke. It all depends on what matters to you.

The advantage of soldiering on in your current business with no additional outside capital is that you get to keep all of the upside. You stay in control, and if you succeed, you own that success. Doing nothing is also the only option that is reversible. At any time, you can revisit the do-nothing option, decide to do something, and seek a buyer. That's not a possibility after a transaction closes.

If all you need is working capital, you can find a lending partner rather than parting with equity. Money is a renewable resource, and there are more ways than one to solve for the problem of finding money to grow. Choosing debt capital over equity capital comes with some risk, but it's a viable option if you would rather not sell just yet. Unfortunately, you won't get the kind of favorable terms that a larger entity like a private equity firm can secure when it takes on debt, and you will likely have to personally guarantee the loan.

The worst part of the do-nothing strategy is that you continue to shoulder all of the risk and own all of the downside. Where are you if your business fails tomorrow and you haven't separated your future from your company's future? All of your work and effort could go away tomorrow, and it happens more than people ever realize. Everything is going really well, and then one day it isn't.

2) Wait Another Year

Another option is to wait until next year. Your company is still on the upside of its growth curve, and tomorrow just might be even better than today. Certainly, betting on the future might pay off and get you a better price. Just remember that opportunities disappear when you don't seize them. And sometimes, successful companies disappear right out from under a CEO who spends too long debating whether now is the right time to sell.

"One more year" can be a trap, and the entrepreneur's eternal optimism can spring it. Without a large dose of optimism, an entrepreneur wouldn't have had the grit to persist through the hard years and risk everything to get where he is. When it comes to selling, though, believing in an even brighter future can come back to haunt him.

Trailing 12-month results are some of the most influential financial metrics you can present to a buyer, and if you are coming out of your best financial year yet, it will be worth more than ever before. In combination with a steady build over time, as opposed to a sudden uptick in last year's earnings and revenue, last year's record results will work to your advantage.

The trouble comes when you are tempted to wait just one more year, in hopes that next year will be even better. Maybe the business brought in $50 million this year, but things are still looking up, and the company seems to be on track for $65 million next year. I very rarely use the word "greedy," but greed really can play a part in a CEO's decision to hang on, year after year, watching the company's fortunes rise, even as he tires of his job and itches to move on. Too often, an unexpected downturn catches him off guard and the opportunity flees. A financial crisis (been there), a major terrorist attack (saw that), an industry crash (got the trophy)—that CEO might spend the next five years building his company back from the ruins. For the ever-optimistic CEO, a hard look at the situation through a pessimist's lens might point to a different path.

3) Find a Strategic Acquirer

The right corporate acquirer can offer a whole suite of advantages. The global economy often favors large companies, so strength in numbers is even more critical. Complementary products, a combined sales force, and a sudden glut of resources can give the combined companies the fuel to grow far faster. A strategic sale is the best option for a company that might not thrive at its current size, but still has lots of value to offer the right buyer. If you are considering this path, there are a few things to watch for.

Meet Bob. He is an executive at your acquirer, and he got to his lofty position because he is highly skilled at climbing the corporate ladder. For years, Bob navigated the bureaucracy, hopping up the chain of command by doing whatever worked. If he needed to throw other people under the bus to get ahead, he rolled with it and never looked back.

Bob is meticulous with expense reports. He ensures everyone who reports to him takes connecting flights whenever the difference in price is more than $400, or he won't sign their expense claims. He is a stickler for the rules and the dress code. The trouble is, he's not all that adept at delivering value to the customer. He doesn't have a vision, he isn't inspiring, and if you're honest with yourself, he would never have landed a job at your old company. Bob can't deliver what you can, which is why your acquirer had to pay for your business.

There are a lot of Bobs in the world, and you know that, but this one . . . this Bob is your new boss.

It's bad enough that you have a boss at all, after being in charge for so many years. And now you have one that can make your daily existence a living nightmare. This is a bad outcome for you personally, one that can be avoided during reverse diligence, if you map out with your acquirer exactly who you will work for (and with). However, Bob is also a danger to your company's culture, no matter who works for him.

The Dominant Culture

Culture fit is more important with a strategic buyer than with any other kind, because culture is pliable. Even if your company becomes a stand-alone subsidiary, separated by many miles from the acquirer's corporate headquarters, your company's culture will often yield to that of your new owners. It's a bit like marriage—you become more like your spouse over time, and if you don't, it doesn't last. Even as both of you change, sometimes one partner changes more. This is especially true in a strategic acquisition—the seller often bends more, to fit the new environment. It's not the managers whose culture has the most impact. Managers come and go. Over the long run, the owner's culture wins.

You will not be able to shield your people from the culture they are walking into, since the acquirer's culture predominates. A culture mismatch with a private equity buyer can create major problems at the strategic level—even break your business. However, with a corporate buyer, the friction that comes from a mismatch can make day-to-day life for your average employee intolerable. If a company that's known for being like a salt mine invests in your business, you know what to expect. But the reverse is also true. If a Baldrige award–winning Best Place to Work invests in your company, that change will be for the better.

Clint Scott ran a boutique health-consulting firm in Austin, Texas, that competed against the bigger firms with a David versus Goliath mentality. By 2002, though, he and his partners concluded that they lacked the financial wherewithal to compete in their space. They started looking for a buyer, one of those behemoths whose brand could lure far more customers.

It was the first time any of the three partners had sold a business, and they did the best they could without professional advisors. The market was frothy, and they knew they could get a good price without an investment banker, so they decided to handle the sale themselves and save on the commission. They narrowed the field to five buyers and finally settled on Chicago-based Arthur J. Gallagher, a publicly traded insurance firm with a billion dollars in revenue.

In negotiating the deal, their first focus was on the immediate purchase price, and their next thought was about the things they needed to put in place to retain key employees—largely to make sure they would make the targets required for the earnout that was tied to the deal. They took almost half of their proceeds in stock and the other half in cash, and they were satisfied with the arrangements—until the integration began.

"I don't believe we did a very good job, and I think that we were naïve. We underestimated the impact it would have on the employees," says Scott.

With the benefit of hindsight, Scott concedes that he should have done more diligence. He should have talked with other companies the buyer had acquired, taking note of the pitfalls and speed bumps they should prepare for. He didn't dig deeper and inquire more because he wanted to keep the sale quiet and respect the deal's confidentiality. In retrospect, that doesn't seem as important.

Right after the close, Scott started to see key staffers leave, even those with financial incentives to stay. They reported feeling more like numbers than human beings, and Scott learned, too late, that his employees worked for him because they believed in his company's mission. Financial incentives certainly mattered, but money wasn't their primary motivator. If he had known that all along, he would have ensured that he made the right decision for all of them, not just for the owners.

In the new culture, little perks became problems. Scott's firm had a casual work environment, where some of the 45 employees wore jeans to work every day, and shorts and flip-flops on Fridays. But the first time the acquirer sent corporate HR down to meet the staff, the rules changed. First, they rolled out a cheesy training video from the 1970s. Scott's crew laughed it off, under standing that they were going through a formal, standardized protocol. However, after the initial chuckle, an HR manager announced that no one could wear jeans on Fridays anymore, let alone on any other day of the week.

"Everybody in the room looked at us like, 'what the hell did you guys just do to us?'" says Scott. "I think our staff felt like we were sell-outs."

Those little things that might seem like minor details were actually disruptive to the team's culture. Scott had, in fact, asked how the acquirers believed they would manage his team, and whether they would lose control of that. The message had been that Arthur J. Gallagher loved what they were doing and would leave them alone to do it, with more resources to serve their clients—and, hopefully, some new clients, too. He also asked who each of his staff would report to. Scott hadn't thought to ask about a dress code, since casual clothing was so commonplace in Austin offices that he took it for granted.

The bigger company's superiority and added sophisti- cation turned out to be an illusion. Scott's clients didn't see any benefits, though the higher profile brand did help to land new clients that wouldn't speak to Scott before he acquired a fancy, familiar logo on his business card. Even though his ser- vices and products hadn't changed, he learned that people buy brands, and that was the main edge his larger competitors had enjoyed prior to the sale. However, even though the merger helped him grow his client base, that didn't compensate for letting down his most critical stakeholders, his employees and the customers who had always stood with him.

After 14 years, it's still hard for him to talk about that sale. Scott left the business right after completing the three-year earnout. If it hadn't been for that financial imperative, he would have left within the first six months. Looking back, there are so many things he wishes he had done, starting with seeking advice from someone who had handled lots of these transactions and knew what questions to ask. He wishes he had thought to ask about the new rules and see whether the acquirer might be willing to bend some. At minimum, he would have liked to have been the one to break the HR regimen to the staff and soften the blow. Above all, he would have opted to slow the merger's implementation, to ease the organizations together more smoothly.

However, those bitter lessons have been put to good use in Scott's subsequent business, a consultancy called CLS Partners. A consulting practice is only as good as its people, and Scott's newfound understanding of what motivates employees has led to a set of priorities that puts employees first, clients second, and vendors third. The culture-driven organization aims to disrupt what Scott calls a stale consulting industry.

The industry is run by people who have operated the same way for the last hundred years, says Scott. "They don't use data or technology to impact their business, so we brought that component into it, and we're trying to disintermediate them from this industry."

While they're busy eliminating the middle-men and working to improve their clients' back-office ecosystem, Scott wants his staff to be rewarded financially, professionally, and personally. That involves a lot of opportunities for personal and professional growth through training and development. By investing in people, he recognizes that most people work at CLS because of what they believe in and who their manager is, not solely because of the number on their paycheck. If he were ever to go through another exit, his top priority would be clear: Protect the staff.

4) Pursue an Insider Sale

If the main reason for a sale is succession planning, you may be looking at an insider sale of some sort, whether it's a seller-financed generational transaction between a parent and a child or a more formally structured handover to all of the employees. An Employee Stock Ownership Plan (ESOP) is an employee benefit plan that holds shares in trust for employees until they leave the company, whereupon the shares are returned or reassigned. ESOPs are the only retirement plans that are allowed to borrow money, so the transaction can either be seller-financed with a seller's note to you from the ESOP or it can be debt-financed. Lots of other forms of employee ownership exist, and starting an ESOP does not necessarily mean the employees own the entire company.

This book will not go into great detail on ESOPs or other insider sales. Its focus is on how to evaluate external buyers and investors and find a good values and culture fit for the future of your business. If you are considering starting an ESOP to hand over ownership to your employees, be aware that they require an extraordinary amount of regulatory work in the area of retirement plan laws and often don't end the way the owner intended. Do diligence.

5) Sell to a Family Office

Unlike a private equity group that invests other people's money, a family office invests its own money. Often these families are looking for businesses they can hold onto for a long time to provide steady income. Family offices vary dramatically from one another based on the personalities of the family members who make the primary decisions and on the family's culture.

I remember walking into a very large multi-generational family office in New York early one morning and finding it already a hub of activity. The children and grandchildren were all engaged in something constructive, whether it was a commercial enterprise, an investment project, or a non-profit that addressed a social challenge. I was very impressed by the extent to which the family put meaning into its wealth and taught the next generation that privilege carries with it a responsibility to keep building value in the world.

In other families, the entrepreneurial spirit dies with the generation that made the fortune. The children are raised in an atmosphere of entitlement, and the family has a clear glide path back down into obscurity. Though family offices are as varied as families themselves, there is one golden rule that holds true: whoever won the gold calls the shots.

As a portfolio company of a family office, you may enjoy a long relationship with your investor. That sense of security can be undermined, however, by the fact that your status is subject to the whims of one or two individuals. There are fewer checks and balances in a family office, compared with a private equity firm that will pass significant decisions through an investment committee. Interpersonal conflict, generational change, or mercurial decision-making can lead to sudden changes of fortune for those who opt for a family office investment.

6) Go Public

When you sell your company through an offering to the public markets, technically that's a sale, but it's not an exit strategy. On a practical level, it's a means of financing. If you are in a capital-intensive industry like mining, going public can dramatically lower your cost of capital. It can also be useful if you aim to grow by acquiring other companies. Still, there are things about running a public company that will make you wish you had never done it.

In the 1980s, engineer John Squires started a computer hardware company that became Conner Peripherals, the fastest-growing manufacturing company of all time. Launched in a garage, the business made the Fortune 500 in five years; a couple of years later, it climbed to Fortune 202.

Squires vividly remembers the company's IPO. Going

public was a heady experience. "We went to Europe," he recalls. "One of the rules of raising money is to try to do it as far away from home as you can. Things look better when they're far away. It's like French wine in California." Meeting with investors in Europe, he started to learn what investors actually look for. After the formal pitch, the one-on-one conversations were all-important.

Once Conner Peripherals was a public company, though, the selling never stopped. The company raised close to a billion dollars through the public markets over the years, and with each dip in the market, the sales effort intensified. Fortunately, his original anchor investor, Finis Conner, was a natural promoter. He got himself on the cover of *Fortune* magazine, and his thought leadership put a spotlight on the brand. That freed Squires to focus on his engineering team.

Still, the pressure was always on to meet projected earnings.

"In the U.S. at least, it's like every quarter is the end of the world," says Squires.

My own experience echoes that. Given the things I enjoyed most about being a CEO, running a public company wasn't fun, because it took all of those good things away.

Data Return went public because we could. We were growing at 40 percent every quarter, and bankers and internet analysts told us the public markets would welcome what we had to offer. The public option was available, which made it very tempting. The more capital we had, the faster we could grow. It let us skip a lot of steps and accelerate what we were already doing to make the business better.

When you file with the SEC to register as a security, you will often receive some unsolicited offers from potential acquirers who know that once your company goes public, it will become much more expensive to buy. In fact, a lot of private equity firms will now run parallel processes, putting their middle-market companies up for sale at the same time as filing to go public, and then taking the route that seems to be working best.

In our case, a public company called Exodus offered about $300 million in stock to buy our company. If I had known what was in store for us as a public company, I may have taken that offer, but without the benefit of hindsight, we turned it down.

By far the biggest cost to me of going public was my ability to focus on making better, faster, cooler things for customers. Instead, I ended up trading in my board shorts and flip-flops for a suit and tie, then living on the road for two years of my life. I would get in a noisy little propeller plane in Des Moines, Iowa, and make my way to an even smaller town in the ice, to make a pitch to a fund manager who probably wasn't going to buy anything. He didn't understand our business, and he was mostly trying to meet with as many CEOs as he could so he could meet his metrics. The work wasn't any fun, and the lifestyle was miserable.

I don't regret rejecting Exodus's offer, because I don't know whether the company would have been the right culture fit, and we ultimately found a terrific acquirer at the end of the journey. But I sometimes wonder whether I might have been able to skip a couple of very hard years if Data Return had never completed an IPO.

7) Find a Financial Buyer

An offer from a financial buyer may look economically equivalent to one from a strategic buyer, but it is actually a completely different animal. Whereas corporate acquirers see your company in terms of the value it can feed into the mothership, financial buyers value your business for what it is today and what it could be tomorrow. When you sell to a financial, your company and brand live on. You probably won't even have to print new business cards. Though a financial buyer may appear to be a single option, it offers a few paths that are quite distinct. Life after a sale to a financial buyer will differ dramatically, depending on how large a rollover you maintain.

Rollover refers to the practice of continuing to hold equity in your own business after a transaction. Depending on the size of your rollover, the outcome of a sale can be dramatically different. There is a common bias among sellers toward overvaluing cash at close and missing the value of a rollover. Money now (the cash you receive on the day of sale) can be dwarfed by money later, when you get the chance to take a second bite at the apple. If a private equity firm sells your company to a new buyer, the growth you've realized since you first sold can make your continued stake worth much more than the original valuation. Many CEOs benefit from windfalls as the value of their remaining equity grows.

You can sell all of your business to a private equity firm, in which case you are probably leaving the company. This option bears some similarity to a strategic sale, in the sense that you no longer have any control over the future of the company.

If you sell 80 percent, the assumption will be that going forward you care only one-fourth as much as your acquirer does about the future of your company. You can decide to leave one day if things don't work out, and your new large majority owners can decide that you are no longer the CEO.

A 60 percent investment from a private equity firm will usually mean that you are staying with the company, hopefully with new resources and help in building up the team around you. If the buyer invested correctly and your company's value grows with the changes you put in place, you stand to make significantly more on the next transaction than you did on the first.

Finally, a minority investment from private equity— 20 percent, for example—is a lower-stakes proposition. You will have a new advisor, who may be helpful and supportive or disruptive and negative. Your life may become easier or more difficult as a result of your new board members, but you still maintain control. The decision to sell a minority equity piece does not require the same level of soul-searching as a majority sale. Still, it is important to understand why you are selling equity and who would make a good advisor.

HANDS-ON VERSUS HANDS-OFF PRIVATE EQUITY

Which of these most closely describes you?

A. I want help and advice from an experienced advisor with fresh eyes. I wish there were someone I could talk to who understands my business problems in context.

B. I'm not sure what help would look like, and I fear an investor would ask ignorant questions. It might be safer to look for a hands-off investor.

C. I have total clarity on where my company is and where it is going. I do not want to be slowed down by explaining and justifying this to someone else. I just want some money for the next phase of my business.

If you answered C), you are best suited for an institutional investor who is prepared to wire you some money and watch from afar as you do what you do best. This will be a private equity firm with a purely financial focus who sees that you are already on the right track and wants to come along for the ride. You know exactly what you're doing, and you feel that if the investors sit back quietly and let you work, they will be glad in the end, when their patience pays off.

Everything will be great with this investor as long as you always make your plan. Their financial-focused lens means they will see you as a hero if you outperform—even if you just got lucky—and they will overreact if you don't hit your numbers. If you miss those projections, expect real consequences. You have asked them to be your ATM, but the agreement is that you will then serve as their ATM in the future. You will live and die by your performance in relation to their expectations, without context or nuance.

If you answered A), you know the value of a real partner as an investor, and much of what follows in this book will help you find someone qualified. In my view, you're making the most of the opportunities that come with a transaction. Help, advice, connections, and money are a lot more valuable as a package than money alone. The money component will mean that the acquirer has a lot invested in the quality of that help and advice.

If you answered B), you are not alone, and I have empathy for your uncertainty. The starting place for many CEOs is that they would rather have an investor who cuts them a check and leaves them alone. They have trouble imagining a hands-on investor who is anything but disruptive to the success of the business. Sometimes this is a well-founded fear.

8) Opt for Hands-On Qualified Private Equity

Someone who has been a CEO or in the founder's chair is in the best position to offer a total partnership package to a fellow chief executive. Understanding your point of view and priorities, a good partner can bring an analytic mind to your financials but also extend that critical thinking to sides of your business that are not as easily quantified. If a potential acquirer only wants to talk about numbers and shies away from the big picture, chances are he is not fully qualified to put his hands on your business.

Most private equity investors have a background in finance and not much else. They are most comfortable talking about financial analytics and tools, because that is the language they understand. Institutional investors previously owned some of my firm's portfolio companies, who needed to adjust somewhat to our style. Out of habit, they would run a board meeting by walking through 50 pages of financial analytics. Compared with business issues like customers or culture—the root of the numbers on the spreadsheet—small line items on a capital expenditures list are of little interest to us. But that's what a lot of private equity firms pay attention to.

Granted, a lot of middle-market companies that still run like small businesses have too few analytics. They don't know where their money is going and what kind of spending creates the best outcomes for them. However, analytics only comprise a small part of what usually needs to change.

An entrepreneurial private equity firm, such as my firm, Satori, has a senior team that has deep entrepreneurial experience. Our favorite portfolio companies have leaders who are open to learning. We have a lot of fun working with CEOs who aren't just looking for a payout, but who really want a partner to help their business get to the next stage of growth. For us, wiring money isn't the fun part. We love the grit of solving big problems and working out a long-term strategy.

When we interview teams from prospective investments, our questions are geared toward understanding the kind of partnership they're looking for and whether that fits with what we love to do: help companies be the best versions of themselves. Questions like, "What do you want board meetings to look like?," "What's your business challenge and how might we help solve it?" and "How often do you want to talk?" can help both sides make expectations clear.

Apart from finding out what prospective investors want and like, it can be useful to discover what they don't like. Ask them what CEOs do to make them unhappy and think about whether you are likely to do those things. In our case, we will be unhappy if our portfolio companies are uninterested in collaborating, act like we don't understand their business, or put us on the mushroom plan (keep us in the dark and feed us manure). You might get more raw and real answers to questions that focus on negative experiences, especially from people who give you generically rosy descriptions of how they envision a potential partnership.

Conversations with entrepreneurial private equity buyers will focus on the same problems you think about every day, and chances are the people you speak with will have had analogous stories to share from their own backgrounds. They can think about your business as it is and as it could be, and they have empathy for what you are going through. Their style will be collaborative rather than dictatorial. (Of course, if you don't want to dig in and work to build the business, this kind of investor is not for you.) You will feel like you have a real partner, as long as you understand your newfound partner's time horizon.

Some private equity buyers have a sunset that will come far sooner than yours will, a lesson that an entrepreneur named Paul Spiegelman learned through experience.

Short-term-itis in Private Equity

Spiegelman has focused his career on culture. While running a healthcare call-center company called Beryl Health, he became convinced that healthy profits flourish in a vigorous culture. That passion led to a sideline in writing books and speaking about culture, all while supporting the families of hundreds of employees by creating a great place to work.

When Spiegelman entered a formal process to sell the business, he received about 20 bids, all for similar amounts of money. As so many of his bidders had met his threshold for price, he was able to make a choice based on who he thought would build the best relationship with his team. In the end he chose a traditional private equity firm that seemed to understand his business. The acquirer introduced Spiegelman to a fantastic CEO who had helmed companies much larger than his own. She shared Spiegelman's conviction that culture was a crucial dimension in the health of a business. They hit it off from the first meeting.

Spiegelman knew that the incoming CEO would run Beryl in a way that was compatible with the company's values. He would have been happy to see her take Beryl's reins while he took on an active chairman role. With the Letter of Intent signed, due diligence began.

BUILD AND FLIP

From the day it buys your company, a traditional private equity firm has one foot out the door. Its executives are already thinking about who they might sell your business to, how much they could be paid for it, and when they might get a distribution. Your business is a baseball card they can't wait to trade in for cash.

At first, the process went according to what Spiegelman had envisioned, with many questions to answer and lots of information exchanged. But before long, the financial questions that came up seemed to have less to do with the future prospects of Beryl Health and more to do with some very short-term interests. After a barrage of questions about the current month's performance, Spiegelman shared his concerns with the incoming CEO. Maybe this was how due diligence always worked—it was Spiegelman's first time accepting any outside capital in his business—but something didn't feel right.

The incoming CEO confessed that she was starting to feel nervous about going forward with the transaction, too. She had never worked with a private equity company before, and she felt that by coming on board, she might be put in a position where she would be forced to make short-sighted decisions that could harm the company's culture. It was a culture she had come to respect during her meetings with Spicgclman.

"It awakened me to the typical business model of private equity. I concluded it wasn't really compatible with the kind of business we had built," says Spiegelman. "It's not to say it was wrong, it's just that it wasn't right for us."

Spiegelman felt that the most valuable outcome from two decades of work was his ability to look back with pride and be able to say that he had created a business that would continue to live up to its values long after he had left. It was important to him that nothing put that core essence at risk or damage his own legacy. If Beryl's culture didn't survive, his sense of accomplishment would die with it, and no amount of money could replace that.

With only a couple of weeks remaining before the closing date, Spiegelman walked away from the deal.

Several factors helped undo Spiegelman's deal, but the biggest was that he and the acquirer were operating with different time horizons. Most private equity firms raise capital from pension funds and other institutional investors. Given its own investors' short horizon, a traditional private equity firm buys into a specific business expecting to sell its stake within five years, on average.

If you were to take on a traditional private equity partner, you would find it clearly stated in its documents the date by which it must sell its stake in your business. You could write that date down on a calendar, and on that day in the future, your company will have been sold on to another owner—one you have no part in choosing if you have left the company. It's not something a private equity buyer advertises to the business it's buying. They will never tell you unless you ask. However, that five-year horizon certainly affects the way the buyer views the business.

When an owner is only in it for a fragment of a business's lifecycle, that leads to something I call "short-term-itis" a pattern of chronic corner-cutting and behavior that shortchanges tomorrow in favor of today, and often reduces investment returns. It puts chief executives in conflict with their investors. While CEOs are trying to achieve a long-term vision, their owners aren't aligned with that timeline. It is critical to understand your investors' or acquirers' horizon and predict their behavior accordingly.

In the next chapter, we will talk about the cure for short-term-itis—conscious capitalism—beginning with how I found a path to a more conscious way of doing business.

TAKEAWAYS

You can still do something when you opt to do nothing. Even if you decide not to sell, it still makes sense to lay a little groundwork for the day when you might rethink the do-nothing strategy. For example, if you connect with a banker who seems to share your worldview, make it a habit to check in a couple of times a year. Think of it as "business dating," which is what bankers like Gary Moon, managing director of Headwaters MB, do with prospective clients.

"A lot of times we know a company for two or three years before they get serious about a transaction," says Gary. "It's great to have a dating period with your investment banker, where you see whether they are thoughtful, judge the culture match between you, and let them demonstrate how well they know your industry. Most CEOs are pretty heads-down in the business, whereas we look at the market all day, every day. We can provide that market information, and in return, we get to know your business better."

To see if your strategies gel, ask the tough questions. As author Alan Webber crisply put it in his book, *Rules of Thumb*, "a good question beats a good answer." While answers often end conversations, questions ignite them. Questions give people permission to reframe their thinking, acknowledge doubt, or kill off a bad idea before it takes hold. They are especially useful when determining whether you and the buyer agree on a strategy for accelerating growth.

It's imperative that you get clarity around strategy, so when you meet with a potential investor, ask questions that make you a little nervous and the investor a little more so: What is your strategy and how do you see us fitting in? What are you going to do with the business after closing? If it goes poorly, what caused it to train wreck? Your aim is to eliminate assumptions and see if there's a sweet spot where your strategy and the buyer's strategy overlap. If there is little or no overlap, that too is useful information.

Work is deeply personal. So is selling. Many of us find meaning through work. Especially for entrepreneurs, our work, and the businesses we create, reflect who we are. When we take on investors, it matters that the personal stuff—our motivations, values, and perceptions—are at least somewhat in-sync, because investors have a profound effect on our spirit and verve as well as our business.

"It's so easy to de-personalize business," says Shawn Nelson, founder of Lovesac, the fast-growing furniture retailer. "We talk about metrics. We talk about performance. But at the end of the day, it's still just people. The investors I collaborate with affect my life in a very visceral way. This is my life, 24 hours a day. This is what I do. Everything from my compensation to my mental well-being is affected by the behavior and disposition of my investors."

CHAPTER FOUR

THE CONSCIOUS SELLER

I spent my childhood outside. My brother and I played in the woods near Fort Worth, and we had gardens. My father is a horticulturist, and he taught us that everything is connected. When you spray Roundup on the plants you call weeds, the rabbits die. When the rabbits die, the coyotes are done. When the coyotes are gone, there's nothing to keep the weasels in check, and you have a weasel problem. Biological systems will self-regulate if left alone, and the mistake people make when they shove the system out of balance comes from short-term thinking.

That basic understanding of ecology underlies the way I approach business. Before the environmental movement monopolized the term "sustainability," that's the word I used for the notion that a business makes itself fit for the future when it works to benefit all of its stakeholders. This view of business has since come to be known as "conscious capitalism." There are a number of dimensions to the philosophy, but all of them are based on one idea: In the long run, when you take care of the ecosystem, the ecosystem will take care of you.

From a leadership perspective, you take responsibility for your employees. This includes fostering a healthy, inspiring culture. As a customer, you are conscientious toward your suppliers. As a business, you do right by your customers. The community as a whole relies on business as well, so you recognize the knock-on effects of your decisions on those around you. All of the economic exhaust from your employees' spent paychecks—the livelihoods of barbers, real estate agents, farmers—they can all be traced back to your company's economic engine. Taxes generated by your business feed into the quality of local schools and police services.

Everything is connected, and the ecosystem will take care of you as long as you put energy into realizing the needs of each of your company's stakeholders. Those connections comprise the life force of business, but they are not always apparent. In fact, it took many years—and the real-world experiences that came with becoming an Army Ranger, managing at Microsoft, and starting two companies—before I fully grasped that business is responsible for all stakeholders, and that those responsibilities are even more resonant when we decide to sell.

In the Rangers: Responsible for Team Members

During my four years in the United States Army Rangers, I experienced an extraordinary culture. Leaders are responsible for the well-being of their team members, end to end. I took responsibility for whether my people were able to perform the mission, but also for whether they had eaten and slept. If our pace didn't allow for sleep or proper food and the team was worn out, I was responsible for keeping everyone motivated. That proved to be great experience when I moved into the business world and I needed to align people around a mission.

Great culture is rooted in a strong sense of belonging. Employees whose identity revolves around their membership in the group take ownership of the company's wants and needs. They understand that the company genuinely cares about their happiness and growth, and by extension, they take responsibility for the well-being of the customer. A sense of belonging can be imprinted through rites of passage, which were part of the culture both in Ranger Battalion and in Microsoft, where I worked next.

The Rangers had an indoctrination program called RIP, which lasted for several weeks. RIP was designed to eliminate candidates by encouraging them to drop out. As we hurled ourselves out of planes, did pushups until we soaked the ground with our sweat, and swam lengths of a pool while wearing heavy boots and backpacks, there was always someone standing nearby and tempting us to give up. The promise of a luxurious posting in Italy was waved in front of us while we weathered incessant physical, mental, and emotional harassment. Lots of people cracked and decided they didn't want to be a Ranger badly enough to take any more of it. The ones who stayed had the Ranger identity locked into their bones like a sense memory, and that identity helped ensure that every Ranger felt deeply responsible for every other team member.

At Microsoft: Responsible for Team Members, Customers, and the Long Term

Microsoft's rite of passage was not a physical test, but it was enough of a trial by fire to push people out of the running. Microsoft in the mid-1990s was one of the hottest companies in the country, and people clamored to work there. We would get thousands of applications for each job posting, and the interview process had to narrow that number down to a handful. Those interviews were like nothing the candidates had ever seen.

If they had claimed on their résumé to have competence in a certain technology, an interviewer would administer adaptive testing on that skillset. Often the interviewer was someone who had helped to write that very software and could plumb the depths of a candidate's knowledge. If it turned out this was something the candidate had glancing contact with in college and didn't really understand from base principles, the candidate would soon give up and drop out of the competition. Some people actually broke down and cried in interviews from the sheer intensity of it all.

However, once candidates made it through that selection process, they were on the team all the way. We had a team that had their minds and hearts fully engaged in building something great, and the strength of their bond with Microsoft meant that they cared about the customer. If customers were having problems because they had set up the product in the wrong way, that wasn't our responsibility, but we made it so. Getting on a plane and going onsite to fix something for a customer was not something we were set up to bill for, but sometimes that was the right thing to do. So we did it.

Overarching the commitment to benefit all stakeholders, conscious capitalism entails embracing a long-term horizon. Many companies make a good show of creating five-year plans, but precious few actually execute them effectively. The winds of short-term trends soon sway them, and they lose sight of the North Star. Microsoft under Bill Gates was extraordinary in its ability to execute long-term strategies, and the whole enterprise thought in five- and ten-year increments.

Their secret was to march relentlessly toward their goal. Incremental progress compounded over time, until seemingly out of the blue, they grabbed the market position they had been aiming for. When they set their sights on a new market, they spent the first couple of years sharpening the ax, and nobody saw it coming until the tree fell. A competitor's product would see a slightly inferior—but free—substitute included in the Microsoft package. Over time, that free product would improve until one day the consumer saw no need to buy the competing product.

Microsoft was a year late in recognizing that the internet would change everything, but when Bill Gates did come to see the full picture, he wasn't slow to act. He didn't set up a committee to debate the issue. He didn't issue a detailed transition plan to shift in the direction of online business. He sent out a single memo to all employees. The memo stated that from that moment, all Microsoft products would be internet-enabled. He didn't know exactly what that meant or how to achieve it—that was our job to figure out—but there would be no exceptions.

A 10,000-person battleship had to make a 90-degree turn, which was my cue to leave Microsoft and start Data Return with some colleagues. Having seen how Microsoft operated long-term, we knew that we were seizing a white space that nobody else would spot until it was too late. Everyone would underestimate Microsoft while it appeared to limp along in obscurity with two or three percent of the market share. But we knew that was just a prelude to a dominant position.

Launching Data Return: Confirmation That All Stakeholders Matter

Our startup used an emerging Microsoft platform to help companies transact business online. Lots of people pooh-poohed the quality of the Microsoft product until one day they turned around and Microsoft was the biggest player in that space. We had a two-year head start by that point, and nobody could catch us.

As a young CEO in my 20s, I had a sense that business

creates value by serving all of its constituencies. However, I didn't see much in the business world that confirmed my intuition. I looked around at the Enrons and WorldComs and started to question whether my ideas about how to treat my stakeholders were naïve. Are companies responsible solely for serving shareholders? Was ruthlessness really the way people succeeded in business? The veteran executives I hired to advise me led me down paths that didn't sit right with me, but I didn't have the language or evidence to defend my values.

Then some time passed. Enron and WorldCom started to unravel. In my petri dish at Data Return, I saw that usually when I acted on my felt sense of how things should be, the results were good. When I listened to the corporate best practices, the results were average. A book titled *First, Break All the Rules*, by Marcus Buckingham and Curt Coffman, also helped give me a broader set of data to confirm my hunch. The outcome of an enormous study by Gallup of more than 80,000 managers at more than 400 companies, the book showed how the best managers find and develop talent in their employees by developing their strengths as individuals. It gave me the confidence to stand by what I felt to be true about long-term results.

Starting Satori: Conscious Capitalism Emerges

During the last few years of my time as CEO of Data Return, I got to know Randy Eisenman, the founder of a smartphone application company called Handango and a partner at

Q Investments. Randy had attended the same Stagen Leadership Course I'd gone through, and he was a fellow member of the Young Presidents' Organization. Randy and I would have lunch every week and often find ourselves discussing the short-sighted way that financial investors operated.

We knew people behaved the way they did because of the system they operated in, and we started to think about what the incentives were that drove destructive, short-term-focused decisions. In the case of the investing business, the structures of investment funds create these behaviors. If your investors have told you they require their money back in three or four years and they don't care about anything but returns, you're going to do what you can to make them happy. Those are your customers.

Randy and I talked about how a private equity firm might fix that. If we could take time off the table, we thought, we could create a different mindset. All of a sudden, the whole operation would shift its focus toward creating the most value over the long term, and that generates very different decisions. We built into our founding documents the ability to partner with a management team for a hundred years if need be.

Randy had started attending an annual retreat hosted by John Mackey, the co-founder of Whole Foods. Those events came to be known as the Conscious Capitalism Summit, and the way of doing business that both Randy and I believed in began to be formalized as a movement. We believe that business is fundamentally good. Free enterprise capitalism is the most powerful engine to create value, and because it is based on a voluntary exchange, it is also the most ethical system.

To paraphrase Mackey, in a profit-centric business, serving stakeholders is simply a way to achieve the larger goal: maximize profits. In a stakeholder-centric business, serving stakeholders *is* the goal, which generates more energy and passion—and often more profit—than the company that solely serves shareholders. A conscious business focuses its energy on meeting the needs of stakeholders, knowing that a healthy ecosystem has more to give back in the long run.

In 2008, Randy and I started our firm, Satori Capital, with an aim to bring a conscious capitalism approach to investing. The idea behind Satori is that there's more to the world than just this quarter's profit, and that in fact, profit is actually a trailing measure of how much value you create for all of your stakeholders. We believe we can affect the future by the way we apply our capital, and that a very long-term view of capitalism will generate better returns, improve the economic lives of stakeholders, and contribute to the community. When enough companies work to serve all stakeholders, the combined effort can be a force for good.

There are three core elements that make our firm different: our time horizon, the background of our senior people, and our practice of conscious capitalism.

First, Satori Capital's differences start in our documents. Where a traditional private equity firm would tie a five- to seven-year selling deadline to its investment, we state that our capital is permanent. The life of our investments is indefinite, which means that any and all issues fall on this side of our horizon. If our portfolio companies have a sell-by date, it is, effectively, "when we're done." We hold onto investments for as long as is appropriate.

That structural freedom allows us to have a long-term mindset and avoid the goofy behaviors that come from a selling deadline.

Secondly, a CEO mindset infuses our entire team, because all of our senior people have been operators. We have all been CEOs or COOs at some point in our lives. That makes our approach radically different from private equity's business-as-usual. We didn't arrive with any bad habits from private equity, because we constructed our ideas directly from on-the-ground experience of how businesses grow. As for our investors, most of them are CEOs like you and me. Our investors and our investees are very similar people, and we see eye-to-eye with both.

To us as entrepreneurs, it was obvious on its face that the old model doesn't work, either in theory or in practice. Randy and I also came from the technology sector, where novel approaches are rewarded rather than feared. In tech, everything is open to a better solution. So that's what we set out to build at Satori— the best solution for family- and founder-owned businesses, based on our vision of the kind of firm we would have liked to have received capital from when we were CEOs.

TRADITIONAL CAREER PATHS

Typically, private equity partners start their careers in investment banking and then go to business school and on into private equity. For about a decade, they learn at the feet of other private equity professionals who have been practicing the same way that everyone else practices.

At no point in that journey is somebody likely to question the way private equity works and decide to follow a path less travelled. The moment just never presents itself.

We much prefer the same CEO to stay on with the business, because even with a solid economic engine in place, the CEO's experience is valuable. Despite what many traditional private equity companies might think, CEOs are not interchangeable units you can just swap out without real consequences. They know how individual employees react to certain types of pressure, and they know how their particular market responds to events. For perhaps twenty years, this founder CEO has put it all on the line and spirited great outcomes through sheer force of will, and her experience often amplifies what we add to the mix.

One of the strategies we have had success with is to pair a founder with someone who loves to do what the founder hates to do. If a founder just wants to be in the office working on the product, we can pair them with an executive who loves sales.

We know that if all our energy goes into getting extraordinary results for all of the stakeholders and we can do it in partnership with a CEO, we build better companies. Over time, better companies are worth more. We might invest in a business for 25 years, if that's what it takes.

Still, we often have exits, and when we do part company, the conditions are favorable. Imagine somebody suddenly knocks on your door and offers to buy your house. The prospective buyer must have a strong reason to cold call you and is probably motivated to offer more than the average home buyer who is touring through every house on the market. In the same way, the right buyer sometimes emerges for a Satori portfolio company that is not really for sale. When that person comes along, we will entertain that conversation, but in the meantime, all of our time and energy goes into building on the strengths of an awesome company and making it bigger.

The third thing that makes Satori different is conscious capitalism. When Randy and I decided to focus our investing strategy on a more distant horizon, we flew around to the usual institutional investors who invest in most of the other private equity funds. We walked them through our philosophy and explained why culture matters. We talked about conscious capitalism—how a company's relationships with customers, employees, suppliers and the community can enrich the investment returns of a business. And we pointed out that none of it works without a long-term mindset, which we could provide with our unique structure.

CATCH AND KEEP

Once we help a portfolio company to grow, it is worth more money, but it might be worth still more just to keep owning it and working to improve results. That puts us in a position where we are ambivalent about selling. If we're making progress, those results compound and patience pays off.

Part of the reason our CEOs built so much value is that they weren't focused on flipping the business. We have the ability to do the same, focusing on helping the company be the best version of itself.

They didn't get it. Part of the problem was that it's hard to put culture in a spreadsheet. They all told us that this soft and fuzzy stuff was cute, but it didn't really matter when it came to investment returns. They rejected the idea that the long-term perspective actually makes a difference, and more than that, they wanted to know exactly when they would see their money back. "I can't tell you how long that's going to be," we said. It was not the answer they were looking for.

It took a few years before people could understand what we were talking about and a few years more before they were willing to listen. If you're doing thought leadership right, that's the kind of resistance you'll meet along the way. You have to be willing to say something that no one else is saying and bear the risk of speaking out. If everyone agrees with you, you haven't said anything new. You also have to be willing to say it over and over again until people don't want to hear it anymore.

Even now that our approach has proven out, many still don't get it. There are a few moments in my life that are preserved in my memory with crystal clarity, and one of them happened when Randy and I went out to raise capital. The man across the table from us said, "You know, with this track record you have, if you would just never talk about this conscious capitalism thing ever again, we could raise so much capital for you. But you've got to stop it."

Randy and I said no.

> The commonly accepted wisdom in business is that nothing really matters beyond money, and that values have no place in this type of decision. The trouble is, that doesn't match the experience of any of the entrepreneurs I've known. When observed reality and received wisdom clash, entrepreneurs choose reality.

After that experience, we turned to the people who could understand our vision: other entrepreneurs. CEOs and ex-CEOs know that how you treat a customer shows up in the value of a business. They understand it deeply because they've lived it and they've seen it at work in their companies for decades. In watching other businesses fail, or in making their own mistakes, they have seen the problems that come with corner-cutting and other short-term behaviors. They know that leadership is not a job for Excel.

As soon as we told our story to those CEOs, we started hearing things like, "Where were you when I sold my business? I wish I had sold it to you, instead of the yahoos I ended up working with." The problems they had with their traditional private equity partners were all tied to short-sighted thinking.

For the CEOs who had sold their businesses, that ship had already sailed, but they recognized the value in our approach, and we heard a lot of people saying, "If I were to start an investment firm, I would do it the way you're doing it, so I want to be an investor."

Little by little, the idea of permanent capital is catching on. Some people structure their investment as a holding company in order to invest for a very long period of time. The legendary success of Berkshire Hathaway owes a lot to its long-term commitment to its portfolio companies. Still, the majority of firms keep hammering away with a "build and flip" mentality and wondering why they aren't getting results.

Many successful CEOs understand the concept of conscious capitalism without using those words. They lean into its principles, but they do so unconsciously. The principles are simply embedded in how they do business. They will talk about their employees, customers, and community without ever using the word "stakeholder." Instead, they will say that the way you treat people matters, and that's the way they built up the value of their business over the last 20 years. Someone who understands that core truth can connect the dots and come to the same conclusions we arrived at in private equity. That's how we ended up with CEOs and family-owned companies both in our portfolio and in our investor pool.

Selling a Business Consciously

The idea that a business is really an interconnected web of stakeholders—a system made possible by those stakeholders—goes against a century of legal history in this country. Beginning with the case of *Dodge v. Ford Motor Company* in 1919, it has been alleged that a business's primary purpose is to maximize profit for shareholders.[1]

The board of directors clearly has a fiduciary responsibility to uphold shareholders' interests. However, we believe that is not a complete perspective. Satori Principal Rugger Burke has published a legal paper outlining how a long-term perspective demands we broaden the purpose of the business to include other components of the company ecosystem.

The implications of placing one stakeholder legally above

---

1 Burke, R. (2014). Sustainability in the Boardroom: Reconsidering fiduciary duty under Revlon in the wake of public benefit corporation legislation. *University of Virginia Law & Business Review, 8*(1), 59 – 83.

all others became more apparent under the subsequent 1986 ruling in *Revlon v. MacAndrews & Forbes Holdings*, where the shareholder-centric view was locked into all transactions when a company's control changes hands. In practical terms, that meant you were no longer allowed to judge a bidder's overall fit with your company, because you were required to take the highest bid.

Revlon is wrong in some important ways, beginning with the assumption that it is even in shareholders' best interests to choose short-term financial gain over the long-term viability of their investment or the well-being of a company they might care about. In the case of a private company, you *are* the shareholder. If your job is to meet the needs of the shareholders, and you are the shareholder, then the right thing to do is whatever you want.

A bid can be high but also unsuitable. It may put your company in the hands of someone who will destroy all of the good will you have created over the course of decades. If the sale goes through, it could result in poorer-quality products for your customers, a cloud of pink slips for your employees when labor is outsourced, or dunning notices from your suppliers, who are no longer paid reliably. In other words, transactions can "benefit" shareholders while recklessly endangering every other stakeholder, and the company that makes this choice is in deep trouble down the road.

In the public markets, where everything hinges on the current quarter, it's much more difficult to think long-term. That's a big part of why I prefer to be in private equity. There's an opportunity in a private company, where the ownership is less diffuse, to make smart, long-term decisions. Our decision engine around business and sale transactions doesn't have to be different and in conflict with our values as humans.

Selling a business without selling out is shorthand for using the tenets of conscious capitalism, especially long-term thinking and a stakeholder mindset, in choosing a buyer for your company: the acquirer who offers the best overall value and maintains the balance in your company's ecosystem will be the best long-term choice, even if the bid comes in only slightly above your threshold.

The Stakeholder Approach

No business is an island. Your business is interconnected with the wider economy and, closer to home, strongly tied to your stakeholders: your investors, customers, vendors, employees, the community, and the environment. Each business has a unique set of stakeholders. For example, in healthcare, patients and payers are distinct stakeholders with separate wants and needs. Just as in a healthy ecosystem where no one species dominates, all of these stakeholders are in competition, and if any one of them has undue primacy, the system falls out of balance.

Some people are surprised that there should be a balance at all, because the visible status quo is a pyramid that puts shareholders on the peak and short-term profits as the top priority—sometimes to the exclusion of everything else. The breakthrough that conscious capitalism represents is that profit is not an objective in itself. It's a lagging measure of value that accumulates when you treat stakeholders well, even if there is a small short-term cost to doing that.

The most natural way to keep all of those stakeholders in balance is not some elaborate juggling act. It stems directly from the start of your business. If your company has a non-financial reason for existing—a purpose, that is—that leads you to prioritize sustainable growth over short-term profit, your decisions are likely to align with all of your stakeholders' interests. It works the other way around as well. A company that has no articulated purpose but has a sufficiently long time horizon will naturally tend to behave consciously, because that is the rational approach.

Conscious capitalism is all about sustainability in a number of different ways. Take one of our portfolio companies, Lovesac. As a college student, founder Shawn Nelson thought it would be fun to create a giant, foam-filled bean bag, eight feet across. The idea took off, and before he knew it, he had a chain of furniture retail stores and he had won a million dollars' worth of investment on a startup-focused reality TV show.

As Nelson matured as an entrepreneur, so did his vision for the company. He invented a direct-to-consumer shippable couch called the Sactional that has a lifetime guarantee for its durability and its mutability—the couch can be reconfigured and the covers washed or replaced. Alongside the products, Nelson developed what he calls the "Designed for Life" philosophy.

Designed for Life has a triple meaning: the ideal product is designed to work with how you want to interact with the things in your physical space and how you live your life in the here and now, but it also refers to a design that's flexible to your changing needs over the course of your life. Finally, the Designed for Life philosophy says that anything you buy should be compatible with life on Earth—that is, it should be recyclable, reusable, and durable enough to stay out of the landfill.

Nelson has made it his life's mission to persuade companies to build products that last and respond to customers' evolving needs so we can consume less and dump less stuff in the garbage. He also wants to inspire consumers to seek out other companies that pursue a Design for Life ethos.

When we met the Lovesac team, Nelson and his colleagues didn't articulate conscious capitalism as one of their guiding principles (they do now), but the only thing they were lacking was the language for it. The company exuded the essence of conscious capitalism, not least by taking a holistic view of the lives of its customers and the lifecycles of its products. After spending a considerable amount of time together, we agreed we were a great fit and decided to partner.

"Having Satori at the table has really changed the dynamic at the board level and given management a more robust sounding board that's more engaged and offers a different mentality from a conscious capitalism standpoint," says Nelson.

CONSCIOUS CAPITALISM CULTURE SHOCK

John Ofenloch, CEO, Ranger Wireless

Before I came to work as the CEO of Ranger Wireless, I spent many years doing restructuring work for private equity firms. I worked for around a dozen firms, and they were completely financially focused. Their cultures centered on squeezing every last dollar out of a company, no matter what you have to do to get it. If I could lay off ten people and save the company an extra $5,000, they would have been all for it.

Satori introduced me to the tenets of conscious capitalism, but there was a significant adjustment period for me as I unlearned all of the assumptions I had come to hold in my previous work environments. The whole tone of the place was radically different from where I came from. I remember marveling at the way people just shared ideas, in a really mellow way, without shouting at each other and dropping the F-bomb every second word. It was hard to believe I was at a private equity firm.

When we first acquired Ranger Wireless, the telecommunications switches it used were becoming obsolete, and the manufacturer wouldn't even sell us an extended warranty. Our choice was either to buy all new switches from the old manufacturer for half a million dollars or to switch to a different source for a fraction of the price. I presented it to Satori, and they agreed it was a no-brainer on a back-of-the-napkin basis, but they had an assignment for me before they would agree to the change.

They told me to come up with a presentation that shows how this affects all of the stakeholders: the employees, the vendors, the customers, and then finally the financial outcomes. At the time I was annoyed because it seemed like they were making unnecessary work for me, but when I actually sat down to work it out, I was impressed with the clarity it gave me. Now I use that process in every big decision for the company.

In a conscious capitalism approach, everyone is valued and everyone's needs count, including senior management. But I was used to the kind of workplaces where 12-hour days are mandatory and they track your movements to make sure you're at your desk. When I came to Ranger, my wife and I agreed that we would both change our lifestyles to spend more time with our daughter and with each other, because there had been no such thing as work-life balance in our family for a long time.

When I sat down for a one-on-one meeting with a Satori managing partner, as we do regularly, he asked me whether I was spending enough time with my family, and if not, what he could do to help me accomplish that goal. Red flags went up in the back of my mind. "We're fine, thank you," I hastened to say, and when I got home I told my wife, "I think they're about to fire me."

If the people I had worked for in the past had said something like, "You spending enough time with the family? You having fun?," that would have been their way of telling me I needed to focus on my job. Months later, after scrambling to work longer hours to try to show that I was committed to the job, I realized the partner wasn't joking. They just know that if their employees are happy, they will stick around longer and the workplace will be better for it, too.

Of course, we have also seen the counter-factual to Love-sac: examples where ownership changes hands and the new owners don't understand the value of the strong culture they have inherited and the trust the company has earned from its stakeholders. The connection between profits and community outreach is not obvious to the new owners, so the outreach gets cut as an unnecessary expense. The owners deem benefits an extravagance—a wasteful budget's low-hanging fruit, which should be whittled away. Efforts that work toward building an organization that delivers long-term value are discarded in favor of a focus on profits right now. The result: the company begins to take more from its stakeholders than it gives.

When Randy and I launched Satori Capital, our experience told us that we would increase the odds of realizing outsized returns if we invested in stakeholder-centered businesses. We set out to support conscious capitalism with our own resources. Once we started meeting with companies across the country, we saw that many more organizations practiced conscious capitalism than we realized. The paradox is that family-owned businesses—and some of the more forward-thinking public companies—don't start community outreach programs and engage deeply with stakeholders simply to drive profits. They put stakeholders at the forefront because that's the way they believe business should work—do the right thing by everyone who participates in the company's ecosystem, and profits follow.

Profit is not a dirty word. If you forget the financial stake-holder, your business will be unhealthy, and having a balance in your stakeholder ecosystem doesn't mean giving equal weight to each. In a consulting business, for example, your employees are probably going to require much more energy and attention than the environment. Other businesses will require that hierarchy to be reversed. But none of the stakeholders—people who affect and are affected by your business—should be ignored.

The moment you start looking for examples, they're everywhere in business. This is not the book to dig into the details of conscious capitalism. But if you are interested in exploring the topic more deeply, read the book *Conscious Capitalism*, by John Mackey and Raj Sisodia. Another great one is *Firms of Endearment*, by David Wolfe, Jag Sheth, and Raj Sisodia. That book takes you through what happens when companies follow the conscious capitalism ethos for 10 years. I'll spoil the plot a little and just say that if you focus your energy on creating value for all of your stakeholders, you will outperform the broader market by 10X.

When you put your energy into creating value and serving the needs of stakeholders, an amazing thing happens. Your business is soon surrounded by groups of people who want it to succeed and will go out of their way to help it do so. The result is that you end up making more money. Let me walk you through why that is the case.

When you start up a relationship with a stakeholder, such as a supplier, you make it clear that you aim to have a true partnership. When the supplier takes you up on that offer, you begin to build trust, as you both make allowances for each other's needs. Your bond means that you support the supplier as its business cycle ebbs and flows. Over the years, you help the supplier get stronger. When you need the supplier to accommodate a special request, it has the capacity to step up.

Of course, the business world is far from a utopia. You might go the extra mile for a new supplier, but when a minor issue arises, the supplier holds you to the letter of the contract. Conscious capitalism doesn't make you a doormat—the stakeholder approach only works when there is reciprocity.

You give stakeholders the benefit of the doubt, making it clear that you are going to treat them as if they already are your partner and that you hope they will do the same for you. Unfortunately, making the first good-faith gesture is often necessary, since many people do not have a trusting outlook as their default mode. They may not really get it, and if that failure to understand persists, then you can deal with their short-sightedness appropriately. But at the outset, they get to make a clear choice. They can choose what kind of relationship they have with you, knowing that your preferred option is a partnership.

If a stakeholder continues to act in bad faith even after you keep doing the right thing, at some point you realize that with this person or company, no good deed goes unpunished. The partnership has to go both ways. When it does, the reciprocity compounds over time, and you both get stronger still.

Many company founders practice the tenets of this stakeholder-centered approach to business. To begin, they tend to care about other things besides money.

If you are the largest employer in a small town, you go to church with your employees. You see your suppliers eating lunch at the Dairy Queen. Your cousin owns the land downstream from your manufacturing plant, and your community depends on the river for its water supply. The result is that you internalize these so-called externalities. They become the bedrock of your company's values.

If you have cultivated those values and used them to grow your company 10X over the past 20 years and you abandon those values when you decide to sell—arguably at the most important moment in your company's history—you will regret it. That big payout will offer small solace when the new owners lay off half of your workforce—your former friends and colleagues—and allow effluent to escape into your community's drinking water.

Those values, which sometimes hover in the background during the day-to-day work of running a business, move into the foreground when it is time to sell. The good news is, when that time arrives, you don't have to abandon the things you value. On the contrary, as I will show in the next chapter, you can and should express them during the selling process.

TAKEAWAYS

To figure out what you value, try putting a price on what you'll lose. Often I am asked how to prepare a company to get the most "value," which is a highbrow way of saying "money." As I've tried to make clear, they are not the same. You care about other things besides money. Think about it this way: You know for sure that on the day after the transaction closes, the buyer is going to fire all of your employees and close down your business. How much more does the buyer have to pay? If you are like the vast majority of CEOs that I know, there isn't a number. Unless it's crazy money where every employee gets years of pay, no amount can compensate for such a loss.

Now we have established that at minimum, you highly value your employees and your legacy. (No doubt, you also value other things.) We have taken the first step. Because once you figure out *what* you value, we can talk about how to get the *most* value.

At its core, conscious capitalism is about sequencing and time horizon. At stakeholder-centered companies, profit is not the point of the pursuit. Profit is a reflection of the value that's created for customers, employees, and other stakeholders. This sequencing often gets reversed in companies that lack any greater purpose than making sure top management's stock options stay in the money.

However, putting stakeholders first does not mean that at companies with a conscience, you'll find team members sitting around holding hands and singing "Kum Ba Yah." On the contrary, they have the grit and the patience to work toward a far longer time horizon than profit-centric companies. They have the stamina to endure a year or two of seemingly little progress, knowing that the big investments they make today will likely deliver a big payoff in the coming years.

Sequencing and time horizon. Get those right, and you've got a stakeholder-focused company that is built for the long run.

CHAPTER FIVE

HOW TO FIND THE RIGHT BUYER

A successful search for the most suitable buyer begins, as ever, with writing down your thoughts before events have a chance to take over. Make a list of the qualities that are important to you in a buyer and how your stakeholders would benefit from those attributes.

Everyone's laundry list of priorities will be different, which is why you can't use someone else's prescription for what you want. For example, President and CEO Paul Poston of Wellington Insurance Group shared the list that he wrote down on a scratch sheet of paper before interviewing prospective buyers for his company. Here's what it looked like.

What matters to me in a partner

- insurance expertise
- highly credible reputation
- high deal flow
- they do what's right for the business, not what's right for the fund
- core value sets around honesty and win-win relationships
- have they done a deal where they screwed management?
- have they done a deal where they were arbitrage betting with multiple funds?
- specialists in our market, not generalists in private equity

Listing your priorities is the starting point for working out the factors that matter in finding the right buyer: homing in on what you want in a buyer; acquiring advice as well as money from potential partners; figuring out the acquirer's plans for your employees; getting real about the fact that this sale really is final; using questions to avoid the "plausible deniability" trap; and ensuring that you tap into your intuition, even as you analyze whether you're making the right call.

Get Clear on What You Want in a Buyer

Imagine a forty-something bachelor who finally decides to get married. He approaches a professional matchmaker, who sets him up with dozens of potential spouses, and after a couple of chaperoned dinners and a coffee with one of them, he proposes. The bachelor never sets foot in his future spouse's house, but her résumé looks great and her bank account balance has the right number of digits.

REVERSE DILIGENCE:

Book a flight to spend a day or two at the acquirer's headquarters. Wander around, meet people and chat with them. Does the experience match the brand you see on their website? Does it feel the same as talking to their team on the phone?

Some companies know exactly what to say and how to say it when they face the world, but those short bursts of image management mask an unhealthy culture.

You may find the place is not anything like what they presented at your first meeting. It may be dark and deadly quiet, with gloomy employees shuffling around looking down at the floor.

Reverse diligence allows you to distinguish a real culture fit from a tightly controlled, public relations performance.

The typical banker-supervised auction process feels a lot like an arranged marriage, where everyone leaves the question of whether this is a truly compatible partnership to chance. The bankers tightly control the meetings to deter the parties from speaking candidly and establishing real trust. Bankers will often try to tell you exactly what to say and how to say it, with a lot of emphasis on what the buyer wants to hear.

It's not unusual to see a letter of intent signed after only a few hours of contact between buyer and seller. After that, there will be more time together going through diligence and answering endless questions for 90 days, but by that time the decision is much harder to unwind. Everybody has already decided your company is getting sold. You may have started to spend the money—in your head, at least—and so you're inclined to discount any red flags.

The antidotes to that rushed process are thoughtful preparation and a commitment (in writing) to reverse diligence. If you've done the work to get clear on who you are and what you want, you'll be able to look very quickly at potential buyers and know whether there is a chance they rate highly on the dimensions you care about. If the answer is no, you can save some time. And if the answer is yes, plan on spending some real time together.

For each potential buyer, you evaluate the effect of that sale on each of your stakeholders, but there is more to it than that. Unless you are planning to throw the buyer your keys and walk away, that buyer is going to be a new stakeholder on the other side of the transaction. When you acquire a new stakeholder, even if that stakeholder is a corporation, you have to understand their wants and needs. You have to know what they want to see happen and what success looks like to them. If you walk into a relationship and your stakeholder wants and needs something that is incompatible with the needs of your other stakeholders or your values, it's not going to end well.

Learning what makes your acquirer tick will help you predict their behavior after the sale, but if you care about your stakeholders, you're also about to care quite genuinely about what your buyer wants and needs. Add them to your stakeholder map as you go through the worksheets at SunnyVanderbeck.com.

Remember: Investors Can Provide Advice as Well as Money

The extent to which sellers want their acquirer to be a true partner varies widely. For some sellers, the money plays a secondary role to the advice. Commercial real estate financier Jack Cohen recapitalized his firm no fewer than six times over the course of 15 years, each time looking for another kind of advisor to steer him toward the next pathway to growth.

Cohen only took on advisors from outside the real estate industry. His logic was to seek out best practices that his industry typically ignored but that might still benefit his business. One of the directors on his board ran a successful computer software business, another was a community banker who was quite risk averse, and another was in private equity and took a more aggressive approach. The healthy tension between them helped Cohen consider his decisions from all angles and grow the business.

As he looked at positioning the business for different types of services, he brought onto the board experts in those new areas—directors who could help him to understand new quirks in the marketplace and unexplored channels, and to execute his plans. Every quarter, he would send out a two-page memo that outlined his strategic initiative and then hold a board meeting to hear his advisors reflect on it.

How did having a team of expert advisors with differing mindsets work? Cohen began with the end clearly in mind. Although he surrounded himself with people who could help him achieve his goals, he did not look to them for a more global direction. He already knew where he wanted to land.

In *Alice in Wonderland*, the rabbit says to Alice, "If you don't know where you're going, any path will get you there." Cohen holds that truth close to his heart, to remind himself to begin with the end in mind, so he knows what he needs and what compromises he can live with to get there. To keep his firm's navigation system pointed to True North, he found that a certain type of partner made the best fit. In his opinion, the biggest conflicts between partners typically arise out of how to prioritize income, equity, and control. (All three are important, but problems surface when partners can't align on which gets precedence.) Cohen's ideal partners valued equity over income, and they prioritized income over control. Each of his recapitalizations had to be consistent with that preference.

During the final recapitalization, Cohen brought on an executive who clearly was fit for the top job, and after 36 years with Cohen Financial, this proved to be his chance to exit. Cohen left while his company was ascending, not least because he acquired investors' wisdom and experience as well as their money.

FOUR SUCCESSFUL CEO TRAITS THAT CAN RUIN A SALE

The personal qualities that made your business great are not always assets when selling. It takes a different skillset and approach to carry out a successful transaction than it does to build an organization over time.

Irrational Optimism

To start a business, entrepreneurs need to compartmentalize their fears. You have to know your industry's mortality rate and how most of those businesses end up failing, so you don't fall into the same trap. Then you need to expel that knowledge from your mind forever, so you can summon the courage to take the risk. Like a gambler on tilt, you put all your chips on seizing a white space in the market that no one else has seen. However, when selling a business, it pays to stare cold, hard reality in the face. There are enough people trying to paint you a rosy picture. Only you can bring the worst-case scenario into the room by asking hard questions. During the sale, leave your rose-colored glasses at home.

Stubborn Independence

Your ability to notice opportunities others can't—and to stand by your convictions when no one else believes in your company—is a strength that brought you to where you are today. It can also leave you blinkered in a sale process. Independent thinking remains an asset, but resisting other people's advice and support or perspective can make you more isolated than you need to be. Advisors like lawyers and bankers have their own incentives, and you would be foolish to ignore what may be motivating their behavior. On the other hand, having seen many transactions, they also have the benefit of a different type of experience and there are times you should listen closely. More than at any other time, your fellow entrepreneurs can be a valuable sounding board through the process. This is not a time to shut out your support network.

Rapid Decisiveness

Most of us feel our way into business and learn by making mistakes. A CEO's day is a series of difficult decisions made with incomplete information, and what most distinguishes a person who can make these decisions effectively is a tolerance for ambiguity. The vast majority of decisions in business deal with issues that come up multiple times, and you get to apply the lessons you learned in the next iteration. Selling your business is an exception, and you don't get to make a snap decision and then fix it later. Few things are more irreversible than the day after closing. Even though it goes against all of your instincts, this is a time to draw out the moment of indecision until you have as many data points as you can possibly collect. Only when you have strong evidence for one direction over another do you make the choice.

A Win-Win Mentality

Building collaborative relationships with stakeholders serves your business well in the long run, as we discuss at length in this book. However, if you have spent years choosing the right kind of employees, fostering conscious relationships with suppliers, and finding customers who appreciate what you do, you may be ill-prepared for the players you will face in a selling process. Be aware that many of the negotiating partners in this game believe win-win approaches are a weakness. Rather than have your good faith taken advantage of, use evidence of short-termism and opportunistic behavior as data points in your decisions. Alternatively, you can choose not to engage at all with win-lose players.

Determine the Acquirer's Plans for Your Employees

An employee who feels valued will care more about your customers. If a new owner does not understand this, they will likely roll a hand grenade or two into your company's culture. A relatively small amount of money invested in culture can lead to a great outcome for customers.

Consider a story I heard about an employee who works in a distribution company's warehouse. The worker saves his paychecks every week for years to make a visit to his family in Bosnia. He hasn't seen them in almost two decades. He manages to scrape together the money, but he needs to take two weeks off for the trip—not a standard request in his line of work—and he is absolutely terrified he will lose his job because of it. He has never taken a substantial unpaid leave, let alone a paid vacation. Days before the trip, his worst fears are confirmed: The boss wants to see him. He's done.

The warehouse worker steps into the CEO's office, pale and nervous, and closes the door.

"I understand you're going to leave town for a couple of weeks," says the CEO.

"Yes, ma'am, I am. I am going to see my family."

She reaches into her desk drawer, pulls out an envelope and hands him two weeks' pay.

"Have a great trip," she says. "Your job will be waiting for you when you get back."

An owner who doesn't understand the value of culture might say the CEO wasted a few thousand dollars that she had no obligation to pay. My perspective is that her move accidentally bought the business millions of dollars' worth of culture at an extreme discount, because that warehouse is going to be a very different place from now on.

In some companies, work pretty much stops at 4:30 p.m. Employees wait for five o'clock, when they can hit the door. But in a company where employees know they are valued, there is a very different relationship to work. No one knows what time it is. They just know they have a stack of orders to get out for customers, and they need to get that right. Four-thirty could roll around and they wouldn't even notice.

Which type of company is your acquirer preparing to own? The company that never trusts its employees enough to show them a human face? Or one where culture matters? There should be no guessing about the plans, and to be sure enough to tell your teammates what they should expect, you have to actually ask the questions. Sit down with the buyer and look at a post-acquisition organizational chart. Seeing the structure of who reports to whom will give you a lot of information about their plans. Take note, of course, of who does not appear at all on that chart.

Don't Forget, a Sale Is Irreversible

Unlike a lot of decisions in business, choosing a buyer is like driving down a highway with hardly any exits. When you start hitting potholes, you can't quickly off-ramp onto another road in search of a smoother ride. There are few course corrections in selling your business. If you make a bad decision and choose the wrong buyer, it will be difficult or impossible to pull a U-turn and get out of the deal.

BUILD A PICTURE OF YOUR COMPANY THE DAY AFTER THE SALE:

- Who is the CEO?
- What is on the website now?
- What is the message to customers?
- Has the team changed?
- What are your priorities now?
- What are your employees doing?
- What are you doing?

Just as marriage is not something to jump into, committing to an acquirer is just not the thing to rush. Of course, once you have enough information to decide, then you need to get on with it. But if you are not used to suspending your judgment for several months to work out a single decision, this will feel very different from other calls you've made. You will have to draw on all of the patience you can muster and work like a mosaic builder piecing together a picture.

That's not to say that the skills you developed as a CEO won't be a vital help to you. A lot of the important work in CEO-land involves fitting together a collection of disparate pieces of data and making meaning out of it—seeing what nobody else can see. If you can pick up a handful of subtle clues and turn that noise into information, noticing trends no one else might notice, you are well on your way to assessing your buyer's suitability. The difference is, as a mosaic builder you will want to form a more complete picture out of all of those pottery shards than you usually do to make sure you catch the nuances of the image rather than just the general outlines.

Sometimes there will be very strong signals from the beginning of the process and the answer will be obvious, particularly if the buyer clashes with everything your company stands for. This saves you a lot of time, because you can quickly rule them out. But more often the buyer is more nuanced, and you've got to pick up little data points here and there to get a real read.

Imagine yourself in a meeting with a private equity guy. You notice he's rude to the waiter and to his assistant but treats you like you're the most important person in the room. It's reasonable to wonder whether his attitude toward you will change once he gets what he wants—namely, your company. Then you have to work with him for the next five years, and so does the rest of your team. Each interaction with a potential buyer helps you to fill in another blank spot in the picture.

What could you conclude from the fact that this private equity guy is dismissive or disdainful of his associates or analysts? If his behavior is materially different from the way you treat the junior people on your team, that may be important information. After all, that person is going to be on your board when this transaction closes, and he may have a fundamentally different value system that informs his view of how to work with employees.

While an investor is not really a "boss," you will still notice a difference when their values are not aligned. Values tend to leak from the new owners into the business, and if you do not see eye to eye with an investor, you may find yourself thwarted at every turn as you try to execute on having a great culture. A first impression will not always show you the underlying values that drive an investor.

Sometimes it helps to dig in a little bit by posing some open-ended questions. You wouldn't be out of line asking: How do you get the most out of a team? What informs the way you lead your firm? If the answer is that the firm combines very high compensation with fear tactics to keep everyone motivated—classic carrot and stick coercion—that will tell you something about how your own employees will experience their workplace under the new leadership.

You would have a very different vision of your company's future if the potential investor responds that his team does its best work when they are inspired to build something greater than themselves. If people have the opportunity to develop their leadership skills as well as to stretch themselves, then they will be better both professionally and personally as a result of the time they spend at the firm. That's a win for the employee, an asset to the firm, and a great outcome for the world in general.

Questions are one source of information, but they won't always give you insight into a leader's character. Some competent leaders don't really know how to talk about what they do. They don't have anything useful to say when you ask them a question with the word "philosophy" or "leadership" in it— their non-answers might lead you to imagine they've never had anyone work for them. But when you watch them with their team, you realize they have a real talent for it. The employees are happy and motivated, you see senior people helping junior staff succeed, and a learning mindset permeates the culture.

If your own company wins awards as a Best Place to Work and offers team-based compensation and the chance to build something cool, an acquisition by a firm that favors the stick over the carrot will not end well. When the new owners cancel your leadership development program for managers and promising staffers because they think the $750,000 annual price tag is a waste, that might look like a smart move—at least over the short run. Five years later, your firm's A-level talent and rising stars have left for opportunities elsewhere and there's a monstrous leadership gap that unleashes a spiral of mounting pressure and declining performance. So it is critical to piece together a clear picture of the boardroom on the day after close and the dominant mindset that will prevail there.

The inevitable moments of stress that come up in a sale are perfect opportunities to see how your prospective owner responds to problems. When something goes wrong in your business, notice whether potential investors have constructive advice for you or just pile on unhelpful criticism.

REMEMBER:

One of the critical abilities an owner must possess is the capacity to distinguish between a market that is getting hammered and a CEO who is steering the ship off course. Your future at the helm of your company may depend on their situational judgment in a downturn.

Even if your transaction is among the fewer than one in ten that go completely smoothly, you can get the same information by asking investors to share their memories of the worst investment of their careers. Ask for the whole story about what went wrong and how they handled it. Does the CEO still work at that company or was he let go? If the investors replaced that CEO, work out how they determined that leadership was the problem, as opposed to collapsing barriers to entry or ultra-low-cost competitors who hammered margins.

After you hear the story of their worst investment, probe a little further to see what they learned from the experience. You might hear that they fired the CEO but now regret it, having seen all of the company's competitors go through the same problems shortly thereafter. They may have learned that when they hire a "professional" to replace a founder CEO, the only improvement they see is in slick-looking reports, and the business continues to suffer.

Ask for the story of their most improved investment. Did they add someone to the leadership that unlocked it or added much-needed perspective? Sometimes you will hear that the founder's skillset was better suited to the role of chair or board member than that of CEO.

A lot of players say whatever they have to say to get the deal locked up, then renegotiate later. To do diligence against that strategy, call people your acquirer has done deals with in the past and ask how different the closing deal was from the letter of intent.

Some differences will be fair and reasoned. If you have represented your business one way but your books say something different, expect those disclosures during diligence to result in reasonable adjustments to the agreement. Other types of about-turn are red flags, especially when they seem to come out of the blue.

It almost takes an anthropologist's inquiring mind to get a good read on a promising buyer. You ask big-picture questions to glean some insight into the buyer's thinking. Observe how he interacts with his senior team and second line. Study the stressors that come up in the process, and note how he handles them. See if he has the confidence to reveal real setbacks and the empathy to learn from them. Do those things, and you increase the odds of finding a good match.

SPEND REAL TIME WITH THE BUYER BEFORE YOU LEAP

Britt Peterson, CEO
Longhorn Health Solutions, an Austin-based
medical supply company

I was around 30 when we started interviewing potential investors. All these companies would come in, and we would drink and eat lunch and talk. They would bring in executives with healthcare experience, and we would sit there while they told us all the mistakes we had made and what they were going to do to change things. I knew we had made mistakes, and I did want to fix them. They were smart people, so their advice was helpful. But sometimes it feels really bad to have people just tell you what you're doing wrong. The conversations were not collaborative, they were just dictating to me.

The main problem was that they were not huge on listening. They were knowers, not learners. Now, I don't want anything to do with knowers who just talk at you. You would say something to them and it was like it just bounced off them. Maybe they just knew exactly what plan they wanted to execute, and they were confident in it, but I didn't get a good feeling from the conversations.

Then I met with Satori, the firm that would ultimately acquire my company. They had many of the same ideas as the knowers from the companies we had interviewed, but they were much more receptive to listening and re-evaluating their opinions based on information they didn't have. They also distinguished themselves in the amount of time they committed to getting to know me and the kinds of conversations we had together.

Sunny came over from Dallas maybe 15 or 20 times and hung out with my family. At that time I had three kids—now I have five—and Sunny came and attended sporting events with us and had a lot of strategic conversations, sharing ideas about how we could grow the business. He asked what we thought we could do with some help, and we discussed the overall health-care landscape and what opportunities were there.

It's my personality to be candid and have honest conversations, and I found a match for that in Sunny. Maybe we shouldn't have been having such talks at that stage in the process, but I felt like I could really be myself and tell the Satori guys what was in my heart.

Every single one of these companies talks about wanting to be a good partner and tells you that they're in for the long haul. What they all mean is three to five years. Satori genuinely means that if it takes fifteen years, it takes fifteen years. We've been through some rough times since that year because the healthcare industry has taken a beating, but their behavior and nature of wanting to help has not changed. It's easy to be a good partner when everything's going great, but when you go through enough with someone, you get to know that it's not an act or a façade. We've had unbelievable support.

Ask the Hard Questions

All of us are hungry for answers, but especially in the selling process, we should pay more attention to questions. As the poet e. e. cummings put it, "Always the beautiful answer who asks a more beautiful question." I've already touched on the importance of using questions to spark meaningful conversations, especially questions that help you glean some insight into how a buyer thinks and what she values. However, the power of asking probing questions to help you dig deep to find the best match warrants a closer look.

SOME QUESTIONS TO ASK A BUYER:

- What is your strategy and how do you see us fitting in it?
- What are you going to do with the business after closing?
- Describe what a successful outcome would look like to you, both financially and day-to-day.
- What are you concerned about?
- If it goes poorly, what will have caused it to fail?

The most difficult questions to ask a buyer end up being the most important ones. They are usually variations on one question: What are you going to do with the business the day after we close?

Too many CEOs follow the ostrich plan, sticking their head in the sand in an unconscious effort to avoid bad news and the responsibility that goes with it. The moment you hear the answer you feared—that a plant will be shut down, say, or one of your departments will not be needed under the new ownership—you no longer have plausible deniability when your employees take you to task over the consequences. Nevertheless, the only way to make a truly informed decision is to understand every aspect of a buyer's motivations and intentions, then identify the conflict points where your goals are not aligned.

As president of MX Logic, Kevin Fallon built a business around a simple internet security product that provided anti-spam and anti-virus protection services for small-to-medium sized businesses. For the customer, there were no hurdles and no disruption: a few minutes was all it took to set up the customer's email to redirect through the MX Logic system for filtering. Kevin describes the highly-motivated sales team he created as "hunter types."

In 2009, when computer security software giant McAfee made an offer, it seemed like a great fit. They set up a deal that included a 20 percent earnout, based on MX Logic's performance after the acquisition. They also negotiated the traditional statement within the buyer's agreement, stipulating that the acquirer would have full control over all aspects of the business after the sale. It was not lost on MX Logic that loss of control could also impede its ability to choose the most effective means of achieving the earnout. However, Fallon reasoned that a win for MX Logic was a win for McAfee. Once the two companies united, their goals would align, and Fallon never questioned whether MX Logic would remain intact.

"On the surface sometimes it looks like, well, what can go wrong? But a lot can go wrong," says Fallon. "To this day it befuddles me, how businesspeople can make these errors."

McAfee had an extensive product line it wanted to cross-sell into MX Logic's large customer base, since cross-selling is much easier than winning over new customers. As soon as the acquisition closed, McAfee redirected the MX Logic sales team to use its customer database to sell the broader spectrum of McAfee products. Sales of the core MX product stopped growing and fell short of the earnout targets, so the MX Logic shareholders lost tens of millions in proceeds.

As Fallon acknowledges, MX Logic could have avoided this misery by asking tough questions. After you assess the buyer's strategy and understand how your business fits into it, the conversation should drill down into a deeper level of detail. Get clarity on the plan for each of the groups in your company. How will finance work? Is marketing going to sit within the business unit or corporate? What's the plan for sales?

If the answer to that last question is that sales will be integrated entirely into the acquirer's team and the team will carry the entire product line, that provides an opportunity for a natural follow-up question: How is our earnout going to work, then? An issue that was previously invisible becomes apparent when both sides hash out the plan's details.

The buyer is not the only person you can question. In the case of MX Logic, if the seller's team had asked around about McAfee's previous acquisitions, it would have found an established pattern of redirecting the acquired sales team and thereby undermining efforts to achieve an earnout.

Listen to Your Heart as Well as Your Head

It's funny how much the analogy of choosing a spouse comes up when you talk to people about how they connected with their business partner or buyer, but they mean different things by it. It could mean that love is blind, and the strangest combinations of people who on paper should never be together end up happily married. It could also mean that without careful consideration, you might pay for your impulsive choice for the rest of your life.

So, is picking a partner a gut thing or a rational decision-making process? The truth is, it's both. A savvy entrepreneur probably knows the answer within the first hour of meeting a potential acquirer. Your intuition is a potent tool, and you should pay attention to your instincts when you spend time with the buyer. How do you feel physically? How do you feel emotionally? That first hour is not enough, though, and you still need to spend the time to make sure your first impressions were right. But be open to the idea that your gut was wrong, too. Use questions and diligence to figure out the rest of the story.

There's an aspect of compatibility that has to do with worldview and focus, and that takes a little longer to assess. What topics spark a buyer's energy and attention? Does the buyer look at your business challenges the same way you do? More importantly, does the buyer focus on solving problems—or are they a spreadsheet enthusiast who is far more comfortable with numbers and dollars?

My read is that the money stuff is a reflection of the business stuff, so I would prefer to talk about the root cause of those numbers. Namely, how the business is doing, why, and what has to happen for it to do even better. Try to figure out how your buyer identifies and approaches problems and whether that approach is going to help you in the long run.

Once your head and heart agree on what sort of buyer you want to pursue, you're ready to get into the shark-infested waters of the acquisition process, the next chapter's subject.

TAKEAWAYS

When you write down the tough questions for buyers, include a few for yourself. Mike McGill, managing director of MHT Partners, a national, middle-market investment bank, pushes sellers to first look in the mirror when they pose their pointed questions. Start by asking yourself why you want what you want. What does it really mean to you, and is it the best thing for your company? Your answers can help pressure-test your motivations and logic.

"In a recent deal I worked on, it was important to the seller that the name of his company persist," McGill recalls. "Is that an emotional need, or does your company name truly hold more value in the marketplace than that of your acquirer? It is useful to objectively assess who has the better brand, and whose is likely to benefit the business. There ought to be a decent business case for your requests, rather than just a vague feeling that if the name of your company changes, then you have somehow sold out."

The advisors' expectations matter, but yours always take precedence. That seems obvious on paper, but it's tough to hold onto when deal fever heats up and you're pushing toward a close. It's a really insidious thing and it's happened to me: as the process moves toward the final stretch, you start to take on other people's expectations. Your wants and priorities suddenly begin to look a lot like theirs. That's understandable. If you're like most entrepreneurs, you don't build companies just to flip them, so you haven't been through a process before. It's tough to keep your sea legs when encountering a gale for the first time.

Just remember: you don't have to care about the things other people care about, such as squeezing out another $5 million when the buyer has already signed on to nearly all of your requests. Get really clear about what's important to you, and make sure the desires and expectations that shape your instructions to the final bidder are yours, not someone else's.

Slow down for yellow lights. In their excellent book on selling, *Let's Get Real or Let's Not Play*, authors Mahan Khalsa and Randy Illig remind us that it's human nature to speed up for yellow lights. However, in the selling process, we must resist that impulse and tap the brakes when green goes to yellow. A yellow light signals situations, questions, and issues that must be fully and honestly investigated to determine if they are really full-stop red lights or whether there's a reasonable chance that with some less-than-major changes, they'll flash green.

Be forewarned: most investment bankers floor it when they see a yellow light. From their point of view, slowing the process to let you put tough questions to the buyer and probe more deeply simply increases the likelihood that the sale will derail. That's certainly a possibility, but not selling is far more preferable than selling to the wrong buyer.

CHAPTER SIX

THE SELLING PROCESS

The moment you enter into a process, you are setting off on a raft into uncharted waters. Nothing in your business experience can really prepare you for the sharks, in their infinite varieties, that swim in these waters. Your advisors are sharks that are looking for a bite, and your acquirers are sharks, too.

Don't let *Jaws* fool you—some types of sharks are harmless and friendly. Nurse sharks pay no attention to people, and leopard sharks are scared of you. Whale sharks look scary but don't even have the ability to bite you. The key is to know what kind of shark you're dealing with and to be wary of the bull shark that will attack you in freshwater where you least expect it, or of the great white, which fellow surfers can warn you about if you bother to ask them.

As you ply these waters, which can quickly turn red as the

aggressive sharks fight for dominance, keep what follows in mind: eleven hard-won insights, which will help you make it to clear, blue water, where a successful deal awaits.

Tell Only Those Who Need to Know

I'm often asked how many people within a company should be told about a sale that is in the works, and the answer is a very small number—around five. Many CEOs would like to be forthcoming with their employees, right from the beginning. They envision having an honest conversation with everyone about what they are doing and why, and what it could mean for the others in the room.

I advise against all-encompassing transparency for a few reasons, beginning with the fact that you really don't know how the sale will affect them. A whole range of outcomes is possible, depending on where the transaction goes. The final time we sold the company I founded, most of my senior management team got promoted. But if you sell the company to the wrong buyer, your team might end up staring at a severance agreement. Another reason to keep quiet: sales fall through all the time, and it's not worth disrupting the company's operations and morale just to introduce a future scenario that may never come to pass.

On the other hand, sometimes sellers are *too* tight-lipped. I have seen people try to run a sale with just their CFO in the loop, but I found that others have to be brought in pretty quickly so you have access to enough information. You can't hide a sale from your executive assistant for long, either. If you don't trust your executive assistant enough to share your plans, that will become a real issue. The other four or five should be very senior people who report to you. The idea is to limit the news to the small group of people who will have the skills and experience to understand what it means without creating an atmosphere of fear.

Somebody at the director level who has never been through a transaction before could well be overwhelmed at the suggestion of a change in ownership. Survival mode ("what about me?") kicks in as you challenge their most fundamental sense of security, right at the base of Maslow's hierarchy of needs. Agitated middle managers will not help you get a good outcome. Besides, fear is contagious, and it can quickly infect your company's culture.

As for the question of when to reveal your plans, tell your small group of insiders as soon as you start getting serious about selling. They may have a useful perspective on the overall plan, so you should loop them in as early as possible.

REMEMBER:

Don't think a group of people who lack a stake in the outcome will help you achieve your dreams. Incentivize the acquisition team to align around the task of selling the company or taking on an investor.

Expect that you will need to draw up retention agreements for those who are helping to make the sale run smoothly, even though this will cost you some money in the transaction—not necessarily dollar for dollar, but the agreements will usually have some effect on the price. It is reasonable for team members to question how the sale will personally affect them. Expect that they will be distracted until they see in writing the kind of severance guarantee they would have, should the new owners let them go within the first year of closing. Once they are reassured that they have a lot of runway no matter what the new owners intend, things will likely go much more smoothly.

As much as your team members are used to entrusting their well-being to you on just the strength of your word, recognize that you may not be around to have their back. Be patient. This may be a moment when you are about to get a $50 million check, but the team member sitting across from you isn't sure whether he is going to keep his job. It's a time to dig deep for as much empathy as you can muster, not least because the transaction may never happen. If the deal falls through, your colleagues will remember how you treated them during their moment of vulnerability.

If none of your colleagues have equity in the company, this sale means something very different for them than it does for you. It means fear, uncertainty, and doubt. They don't know who their new boss will be or whether they will even have a job. Worst of all (from their point of view), they don't get to participate in the decision. Assuming they like their jobs, the starting place for all employees is to believe that a change in ownership is bad.

Some of these issues are solvable. If someone on your team deserves a piece of the pie, you can get that done, one way or another, before the sales process goes any further. If you've been meaning to give your management team equity but you've been kicking that can down the road, now is the time to make sure it gets done. Any further delay could blow up in your face, probably in a way that you can't even see right now.

Hit Your Numbers

If there's ever a time for your engine to run smoothly, it's when you're trying to sell your car. You do not want to have to tell a customer, "Oh, that knocking sound? It does that sometimes but then it goes away. Don't worry." Any potential buyer will listen to your engine knock and demand a discount.

The same principle applies when you miss your projections, just when a buyer is doing due diligence. If you tell an investor that you had $6 million in profit last year and you're expecting seven million this year, the last thing she wants to hear in November is the sound of you walking that number back down. A shortfall calls into question the future of the business, and the investor will use it against you.

When you say, "This one account fell through, but it's all temporary—it's a one-time thing and we'll pick it up in Q1," the investor hears, "I stretched my numbers." The investor will assume that you pulled some revenue in to get the numbers up and that you overreached on your financial plan—maybe you weren't that good at planning anyway—and probably biased up to tell him the best story. That $40 million price you settled on is called into question, because now you're talking about a lower starting place, which means a lower return on his investment. It would be fair for an investor to ask why they should eat that difference in returns when it was your business that didn't perform.

There are some situations when excuses don't cut it and pointing fingers doesn't help. Imagine you sell your house and promise that it will be landscaped when the new family moves in, but the landscaper does a bad job and the trees all die. You can't expect to be paid the same amount for the house when your side of the bargain didn't come through.

Get Organized

Businesses often falter in the year they're going through a sale because selling sucks up a lot of energy and bandwidth. You need to prepare for a multi-month stretch where everyone on your senior team will have two jobs at once, which will be tough on them. The less organized your company, the greater the likelihood that it will hit the wall.

The company that is locked and loaded, with well-documented processes and data on everything it does, will have a much easier time of enduring due diligence. The acquirer will ask for 10 year old numbers, and your CFO will call up the relevant file, hit "Send," and get back to the core work of running your company's financials.

On the other end of the spectrum is the company with none of those smooth-running systems and no CFO. The acquirer will ask for 10 year old numbers, and your finance guys will have to go back and recover them—a major time sink. That's when due diligence can derail a company's performance by pulling people away from the day-to-day work of running the business.

A CEO once told me there are buyers who will load up due diligence tasks in order to break the company, just to get a better price. That seems awfully short-sighted because they damage the very thing they want to buy, but I can believe it happens. Don't let it. If something's going to fall apart, let it be the sale process, not your company. At the same time, it is entirely reasonable for an acquirer or investor to ask lots of questions and expect answers.

On a pilot's checklist for navigating a systems failure, the first item is "Fly the plane." The threat posed by a flaming jet engine or an electrical blackout consumes all of the pilot's attention. The pilot needs reminding that any kind of emergency fix requires—at minimum—that the plane stay in the air. The same holds true for high-flying entrepreneurs. Even when you're in the middle of due diligence, run your business like there's no closing on the horizon. And do not (do not!) allow that emergency light on your instrument panel to start flashing red, signalling that you just missed your projections. Don't let yourself get distracted.

Consider Running a Limited Process

"It's a tough thing to even talk about, because if you do, it's like, 'Boo, hoo, hoo. Take your big bag of money and shut the hell up,'" says Cory Janssen. He maintains he has been less happy since he sold his business than he was before the sale. He also has difficulty finding people who can relate to his disappointment, even in his network of entrepreneurs.

While confusion and regret are possible outcomes of a sale, they do not define everyone's post-sale experience. So, what makes the difference between one CEO who comes out of a sale fundamentally at peace with the decisions he made and another, like Janssen, who struggles in the aftermath?

REMEMBER:

Your advisors work for you, not the other way around. The moment you feel as if you are being marched along a path that doesn't fit your way of thinking, you have every right to pull rank and, in a pinch, to pull the plug.

A lot of the problems stem from the formal sale process. People who enter into that process often get carried away by the force of its momentum. In contrast, those who follow a more limited process—or even talk to one buyer at a time—strike me as happier on average with the result.

A formal sale process, which uses an auction to select a

buyer, is designed to accomplish two goals: maximize the price and maximize the chance of closing. It achieves those things very efficiently. To win the highest possible price, you only need one acquirer with a crazy idea of what your business is worth, so the banker who sends your package to many prospects is more likely to flush that buyer out of the woodwork.

On the other hand, if anything matters to you beyond price and closing, you might still choose a formal process, but you will have to expend a lot of energy to fight the system's inertia and make those other priorities heard. You may have to assert yourself several times before your commitment to the things that matter becomes clear to others.

Write down, in order of importance, your criteria for evaluating potential acquirers. Even if your priorities are clear in your own head, it is crucial to put them in writing to demonstrate that you are deeply serious. Otherwise, advisors assume that as soon as a great bid comes in the door, those priorities will fly out the window.

At Satori Capital, we rarely even look at companies that are in a traditional process because our goal is to pay a fair price for a business that seamlessly aligns with our values. Without a doubt, some qualifying businesses will launch a formal auction, but that system minimizes our exposure to the management team. It takes real time to dig in and discover whether we align with a seller's culture, goals, and plans. By contrast, the process discourages meaningful interaction between the buyer and seller. So we usually don't play.

Lots of smart CEOs opt out of formal auctions. The

alternative is to run a more limited process, which allows you to spend plenty of time with your acquirer, establish whether there is real alignment, and come up with creative solutions that suit you. The same advisors who are accustomed to using an auction to cast a wide net can also help you hand-pick five or ten buyers for a more meaningful exchange. Some sellers choose to engage deeply with one prospect at a time, often because the buyer has personally approached them.

When Garry Waldrum sold his LED video display company, TS Sports, to Panasonic, he had already spent two years talking to potential buyers one by one and politely declining their offers. None of them seemed to have a good sense of the market he was in, and they didn't buy into Waldrum's ideas for growing TS Sports, given access to deeper pockets. When Panasonic gave those plans the nod—and even offered Waldrum a place on its acquisitions team so he could add more companies to the team—he knew he'd found the right fit.

"A couple of my advisors said I could get another million dollars," recalls Waldrum. "My answer was, 'It ain't all about the money.'"

Waldrum spent the next year preparing for the transition. The new home Waldrum furnished for his company's staff was well appointed before they moved in. It took some hard and expensive bargaining, but all of his employee's vacation days and insurance carried over to the new company.

In a large, hierarchical company like Panasonic, seniority is an extremely valuable asset, and Waldrum did not want his long-serving employees to have to start over when they moved to their acquirer. He negotiated that each year of service to TS Sports would count as a year of service to Panasonic. The pride he felt while watching Panasonic award one of his loyal employees a 20-year service pin—after only 18 months with the company—confirmed for Waldrum that he had done the right thing.

Most of us feel a mixture of loss and liberation on the day our company changes hands, but the important thing is to ensure that in the years and decades afterward, those feelings coalesce into a sense of accomplishment. If you make decisions during the sale that are true to your values, you are likely to look back with deep gratitude on the years you owned your company.

No Heroics

Imagine you are a buyer choosing between two businesses with identical growth and profit. Company A has a phenomenal leader, and the business is outperforming everyone in the industry. The CEO knows the intimate workings of every department and keeps track of everything that goes on in the business. Company B, on the other hand, has a lazy CEO. He takes four months of vacation every year and glances at periodic reports on the company's progress. Which company would you prefer to buy?

REMEMBER:

Any component of the business that might be lost as the result of a transaction, including a key customer, a major supplier, or a talented executive, will raise a red flag during due diligence.

As someone who regularly sits on the buyer's side of the table in meetings with CEOs, I have seen my share of sub-par presentations. Companies that drive down their value during a sales process rarely seem to understand the factors that contribute to their failure. At the root of their mistake is a false impression of what buyers look for.

Celebrating their executive team's heroics is one of the most common miscalculations CEOs make during a sale. When a buyer hears about the extraordinary measures that fueled a company's growth and about the prodigious talents of its executive team, the company's value does not rise in his estimation—it falls.

If CEO A is involved in every aspect of the business, it's very likely that key information lives in his head and never makes it to paper. The company's success depends entirely on the CEO staying—and staying engaged—in the business after closing. The "lazy" CEO B, in contrast, has shifted from hands-on mode to more of an ownership role, so there is less risk that he will complicate the transition to new ownership. A buyer will put a premium on Company B because it can run perfectly well without its chief executive, whereas Company A leans heavily on its leader.

Another thing that dilutes a company's value in the eyes of a buyer: anecdotal evidence instead of data. By all means, tell your company's story and link that story with the ways in which your unique strategy works. The key to telling an effective story, however, is in knowing the difference between a compelling narrative and a tale that is meant to mask hard facts.

Diligence is a learning process for both parties. Be open to answering questions and remember to ask your own. If you get a CPA involved early on and have clean financial statements on hand, diligence will go more smoothly and quickly. Anticipate what comes next. Organize your documents and data ahead of any diligence requests so you can focus on the things that matter most to you.

If a buyer requests your last five years of projections and the actuals to those projections, he will be interested in the content of those documents but even more interested in the fact of their existence. Many young companies avoid the practice of annual budgeting, even as they grow to employ upwards of 200 people. I have heard all kinds of excuses for this. Some CEOs think they can keep everything in their heads, and others feel their business is too volatile to make projections. Just remember that if you cannot make a one-year forward projection, then you also cannot help the buyer become comfortable with the business's future. To a buyer, your habit of drawing up a budget every year implies discipline and purpose.

If those files do not immediately arrive, the buyer will assign meaning to that fact. He will either assume that you are not professional enough to create a budget every year or suspect that wishful optimism infuses your projections. In any case, the prompt delivery of those budget documents will reflect much better on the company than a story about how the company pulled together to accomplish a last-minute customer project.

Build Your Credibility (That's What Buyers Care About)

Imagine taking a realtor's tour of a house that's for sale and finding Cheetos lodged in the couch or tripping on the Legos strewn across the floor. Even though the contents of the house are not part of the sale, you would likely leave with an unsavory impression of the property and its owners.

In the same way, your facilities should be spotless when a buyer walks through them. A buyer might check behind a door or in a corner of the plant, and when they find it clean, they will make meaning of that. In their minds, a company that doesn't take pride in keeping a clean, well-lit workplace might take the same undisciplined approach to product quality or culture.

The company records should be just as pristine. Every clear and concise answer you can give in response to questions about your records will put a chip in your credibility pile. You could use your credibility chips to buy a few little leaps of faith about mysterious line items or transactions, or you could use it to bolster the buyer's confidence in your predictions. With enough credibility in your account, the buyer's default position will likely be to give you the benefit of the doubt on less-than-crisp answers to questions about the future. Either way, in the buyer's eyes, everything that builds the case for your credibility also drives up the value of your business.

REMEMBER:

Acquirers are investing in you and your team every bit as much as they invest in your company or product. That makes it important to be as genuine and authentic as you can in conversations with buyers.

When something about the current business isn't too pretty, just say it's not too pretty. If you stretch the truth, your caginess is going to show and draw much more suspicion than whatever small concern you were trying to gloss over.

A buyer will walk into every meeting intending to separate fact from fiction. Their job is to guard against swallowing a fiction—or anything that smells like one. If you want an acquirer to buy into your vision of your company's future, the most powerful point in your favor is the credibility you build in disclosing your past—miscues as well as breakthroughs. The careful assessment that went into your current projections is only as good as the accuracy or defensibility of your previous projections.

Nothing kicks off an acquisition process better than a first impression that signals competence. You create that impression by showing that your team is organized and by clearly explaining how the business works and how it will grow. An organized presentation that marshals facts to support every claim will go a long way toward setting a tone of transparency and authenticity.

A buyer's next most important job is to predict the future, because that's what they're betting on. Whenever you tell them about yesterday's performance, they will translate your words into what it all means for tomorrow. For example, if your historical growth rate has been 12 percent, be prepared for some raised eyebrows when you claim that next year it will climb to 20 percent. However, if you've established real credibility about what happened, buyers will find you far more credible when the conversation turns to what *will* happen.

Go for the Good Deal, Not the "Fair" Deal

Congratulations. You've landed on the right buyer, and they have proven to be a great fit for all of your stakeholders. Exhaustive due diligence has shown that they meet all of your big picture needs, including your financial outcome. All you have to do now is ride out the process and refrain from messing it up.

But somehow, a couple of months later, you're staring at a term in the buyer's contract that really rankles. What's worse, your attorney is making a stink about it—the term is unfair, and it's starting to seem like a symbol of the buyer's bad faith. The process is moving in fast-forward, and its intensity leads you to start second-guessing your own judgment. Perhaps these acquirers aren't the honest dealers you thought they were. It feels like your pride is at stake. Maybe you should blow up the deal and walk away.

Close the deal.

A good deal is not the same as a fair deal, and you won't regret settling for a good one. When the negotiations over those final terms start to heat up, it can be easy to lose sight of the big picture. Ten years from now, it will not make you sad—or even angry—that your escrow calculation was unfair. The banker who seems so vexed about it right now won't remember it either. Your life will not be different. However, if you let your emotions rule you now, at the eleventh hour, when fifteen years of your life's work is at stake, you will regret that bitterly. Take the good deal.

Commit to Yourself in Writing

If you think you might be prone to losing perspective when an injustice arises, guard against it now by writing down your priorities. That critical move saved Cory Janssen's deal when he sold his digital media company Investopedia to Forbes in 2006.

Janssen and his business partner decided to embark on a formal sale process, and their banker provided them with a range of possible valuations. They then worked out a threshold number and wrote it down. Rather than base that number on the banker's estimates or even on their own assessment of what their business was worth, they listed the things they wanted and added them up. Janssen wanted a substantial sum to seed his next business, a certain amount for a new house, and a nest egg for his children. Then, they put the paper in an envelope and sealed it.

After about twenty phone calls with prospective buyers, roughly ten in-person meetings, and an in-depth discussion about the top three contenders, Forbes prevailed as Investopedia's preferred buyer. Then five months in—just days away from closing the deal—their negotiating partners tried to switch something on them. Janssen was furious. A large part of him wanted to walk away.

It was time to open the envelope. What was it they had wanted from this process, which now seemed so fraught with frustration? "We picked up this piece of paper and said, 'Wait a minute, okay, five months ago we were happy with this number. We're well over that number now. We have got to remember how much has changed in just five months,'" recalls Janssen.

Seeing that magic number, which actually grew over the course of the sales process, brought him back to reality. So much had changed since the decision to sell, he just needed to hit "pause" and return to his original definition of success. They were so close—all they had to do was swallow their pride and sign on the dotted line. Janssen's note to his future self was the critical tool that saved the deal.

All this is true for non-financial objectives, too. If you write down what success looks like for all your stakeholders, you can refer back to those priorities whenever you feel you might be losing sight of what matters.

Don't Sweat the Small Stuff

Small details have a way of expanding to fill your field of vision, and your advisors will exacerbate the situation. As strong as their expertise might be, the advisors' weakness lies in judging the materiality of a problem. When a risk is brought up, ask your advisors how big its impact would really be and whether they have ever seen an example of it happening.

It can also be tempting to get hung up on the last dollar. Will that dollar—or even those last three million dollars— make a long-term difference to you? Take it from the CEOs interviewed for this book, who all answered the following question: If you had taken home 10 percent more from the sale of your company, what would be different now in your life? And if you had taken home 10 percent less, what then?

The CEOs who contributed their thoughts to this book are a diverse bunch, representing a wide range of industries and types of transactions. There are vast differences in the outcomes of their business sales, running the gamut from pride to regret. However, on this question, they spoke with one voice: Nothing would be different. Nobody wants to leave money on the table, but when the picture zooms out and the ensuing years provide perspective, that last 10 or 20 percent won't matter. What *will* make a difference is what happens the day after closing.

If you find that perfect fit, then, don't trade all that

upside—your success and happiness—to quibble over trivial terms or that last dollar. Close the deal—fast. Time matters. The longer the close, the more likely a problem will flare up before that contract is finalized. There is no such thing as a 99 percent completed transaction, and a sale that almost happens but never does—especially when it promises to be a perfect fit—can haunt you for years. Many CEOs can tell you their version of what I call the Day of the Long Faces, when they almost struck the perfect deal, before the fates intervened.

If I could go back to the summer of 2001, before the day when the fax machine went silent, I would teach my younger self about the pace of M&A. I would tell the younger me to do everything in my power to close the sale to Compaq in a hurry. I know, looking back, that there were plenty of opportunities to move the sale along. I simply didn't understand the need for speed. There couldn't have been a better fit for my company, but on September 3, that option vanished.

Consider the "Spirit of the Deal"

If you and the acquirer are well aligned on the sale before the transaction is formalized, you may want to consider drawing up a "spirit of the deal" document. The idea is to help everyone avoid getting bogged down in the details of the legal documents and the little battles that break out over terms. The "spirit of the deal" keeps both camps' eyes on the overall aim of the transaction by documenting, in one or two pages, the main principles that will guide your agreement. That way, when you inevitably run into an issue—perhaps one brought to light by your advisors—you and the buyer can refer your attorneys back to what both sides really want to achieve with this deal, and they can see the way forward. Remember that lawyers are not there to make a deal. Businesspeople make the deal, and their lawyers implement that deal in writing.

A "spirit of the deal" document is entirely different in tone from a letter of intent, in that it summons both sides' values and establishes an informal code of conduct for completing the deal. Possible terms include, "We're always going to give each other the benefit of the doubt," or "We're trying to be fair to all stakeholders in this transaction," or "If something happens before close, it's a seller liability, but after close it's a buyer liability."

If those are the principles that will guide the sale's consummation, the lawyers may quickly delete a term in the contract that creates value for one party at the expense of the other and insert a term that works for everyone. Referring your advisors and attorneys to the broader principles at work in the sale can be a kinder way to remind them you're here to get the deal done, not to win some petty victories over people you're going to work with for years into the future.

Add Value by Hiring Valuable Advisors

Perhaps it's self-evident, but it should be said: Hire advisors who will give you valuable advice. This is not a moment to shop for a discount. Mergers and acquisitions is a specialized skill, so the corporate attorney who knows your business is not the right person for this challenge. An M&A lawyer will have seen many more transactions than he has—if he has seen any at all.

As an investor now with Satori, if I find myself sitting across the table from a family attorney representing our prospective portfolio company, I know all of us—including the seller—are in for a wild ride. We'll probably get better terms, but the process is going to be very painful, and both sides will waste time on what should be standardized terms.

Long ago, people figured out a way to solve some of a sale's chronic challenges in a way that is equitable to both sides. Their solutions have evolved into terms that now are standard in every contract. Unfortunately, inexperienced attorneys tend to miss the issues that we should discuss with a potential buyer. Instead, they often end up renegotiating the very issues that most contracts have already resolved. When there is a professional M&A attorney in the room, we know we'll have to negotiate a number of items, but those items will matter.

What goes for attorneys applies to investment bankers as well. In one instance, when we were selling Data Return for the first time, we ended up firing an investment banker and hiring another one, even though under the terms of the first contract we had to pay for both. From a purely financial angle, it's very difficult to make that decision, because one investment banker alone is very expensive. However, a great banker can raise the value of your sale by much more than the value of his fee, so in our case it was still worth the trade.

After you successfully navigate the twists and turns of an acquisition proccss and signing day has come and gone, there is one last task to tackle, which I cover in the final chapter. For many CEOs, it will be the toughest part of the journey: reckoning with the day after close.

TAKEAWAYS

Make sure the decision-maker is in the room. The first time we put Data Return up for sale, we got a very impressive offer from a major telecom company. As the negotiations began to heat up, I grew increasingly concerned that the company's CEO wasn't participating in the discussions. Our investment bankers told us not to worry, this is how it works with big companies. We had their corporate development group and their business unit heads in the room, and that's what mattered. I was just in my late twenties, and I took their advice. Begrudgingly, I stopped worrying. That was a mistake: the CEO didn't even know about the sale.

When the company's executives finally got their ducks in a row and took the deal to him, he threw them out of his office. He had just drained many millions from the budget, funding all the other stuff they wanted. End of conversation—he wasn't about to spend another dollar on acquiring us. With that, six months of effort just vanished.

Our inability to correct for the CEO's absence delivered a lesson that I have carried with me: if the person who owns the "D" is nowhere to be found in the selling process, you don't have a sale.

Get a reference. As I have previously pointed out, the private equity fund that wants to invest in your business is potentially your partner, not just your buyer. You need to suss out not only whether they understand your market and business, but what kind of people they are, whether they will be good to work with and most especially, whether their interests align with yours. That's where management references come in.

"Always, always ask for management references," says Jane Greyf, an attorney with Goodwin Procter LLP's private equity team. "You should be well-versed in that particular fund's reputation on the street and how well they are reputed to work with management.

"Most private equity funds should have people you can talk to—people who they've taken through a turn and then sold," Greyf continues. "It's best to talk to those who are no longer owned by the fund, partly because they don't have to tell you anything nice, but also because they can speak about the second exit stage. It is extremely important to look at how you are going to be treated on the second exit stage—how much of an influence you will have and how your financial outcome might compare to the one the fund has depicted in their sales job."

Don't get pregnant. When you've spent two decades bringing your vision to life, selling can feel like parting with your first-born. It can get very emotional, very fast. Many conflicting feelings—concern and desire, excitement and sorrow—start to swirl. You can get into trouble if you're not self-aware, especially if a lot of your net worth is tied up in the business. As M&A advisor Fred Thiel points out, the more you expect the sale to go through, the more those emotions intensify.

"It's referred to as being 'pregnant,'" says Thiel. "If they know you don't have a lot of liquid net worth, an acquirer might egg you on to dream about the home you could buy with the check they'll give you. Once you're hooked on that image, they might come back and lower their bid, knowing that you will have a newfound dread of not getting a deal done. The fear of losing that dream home you never owned in the first place can affect your perception of the company's valuation."

Remember that advice I gave about writing down your threshold number and sticking it in an envelope? When deal fever heats up and your emotions start to surge, go back and read the number. It will help you regain your clarity.

Money matters, but it won't make you happy. Once you cross your money threshold, a much deeper sense of satisfaction comes from knowing that you have done right by your stakeholders. There is an enduring pride in having taken care of the ecosystem that helped your business grow into what it has become. Your non-financial objectives for the sale—addressing the needs of all the people who contribute to the business's success—will likely become increasingly important to you in the years after close.

CHAPTER SEVEN

THE DAY AFTER THE CLOSE

When I think back to the months after my last day at the company I founded and built, I can't really explain my actions. I was supposed to serve 90 days of transition, but far sooner than that, my acquirer saw that I wasn't actually involved in any of the business processes. As a CEO, I wanted to build a business that could run without me. Now that it was proven, I wasn't needed. I don't know whether I would have been fully prepared to exit after three months of transition, but I certainly wasn't prepared when I did leave after just a few weeks.

The next Monday came, and I didn't have a clear idea of what to do. I remember spending a lot of time just doing *stuff*.

I remember mentally flirting with the idea of going out to explore the world. I read about a company that offered a

180-day walk through South and Central America. For about ten minutes, I imagined how great it would be to hike in Patagonia. But I just couldn't put myself in that mindset. I had been a CEO since I was 23 and a Ranger before that. I lacked a mental map for dealing with empty time. Humans generally don't do very well when we lack something to really work on— something that summons our imagination and grit. It's a funny thing about the human condition that we're happiest when we are struggling.

During those months, I can't tell you why I slept in on Saturday and Sunday but not on Tuesday. There was no reason for it but habit. For six months, there was little reason for me to stay on top of email, but I kept at it and started volunteering for stuff. My day filled up with meetings that lacked value, and I ended up just as busy as I had been when I was a CEO. This was supposed to be different. I knew I had a project starting in six months—the launch of Satori Capital—so for me the transition period had light at the end of the tunnel. Not everyone is so lucky. The CEOs we have followed in this book went on to have a wide range of post-sale experiences. Let's take a look at where they are now.

Keeping an Owner's Mindset (Even When You No Longer Own)

For a long time, as a company builder, the only thing you truly own in your business is your founder's equity. You bear its full weight. Through the years, as your company surmounts some obstacles and succumbs to others, you own every leap forward and every setback. Then, as the company's growth arcs steeply upward and your risk begins to pay off, that equity is worth something to other people. However, at that point, much of your identity is tied up in your equity. Selling your business can feel like losing a part of yourself. But only if you let it.

Even if you have sold off a big part of your stake, you don't have to lose that ownership mindset. We've discussed the way some employees have an ownership mentality even if they lack an equity stake, whereas others with shares somehow don't seem as invested. The same can be true of a founder who has sold a lot of equity. Shawn Nelson, who founded a Satori portfolio company, has no illusions about his investors owning the vast majority of Lovesac, but he never hesitates to call it "my company."

"I can choose to feel like an employee, but I will never think about it that way. I will think of it as my company, and I will behave as if it's my company," says Nelson.

As for losing control of his company, he doesn't feel that he has. You don't need to own a company to control it, he says, you just have to be awesome. Take Michael Jordan: He neither owned the Chicago Bulls nor was he the coach, but he controlled that team by being the best.

"If you're awesome, it's going to be very rare that anybody can really take control away from you unless you get yourself wound up in a mental dither about ownership and dilution and board control. Just be awesome, and it's very hard to argue with that," says Nelson.

He compares his company and its investors to a kite and a string. A kite might blow around in a windstorm, but it will fly higher and more steadily with a skillful hand guiding the line. Those hands are the veteran influence of his board of directors, who helped him prepare for his next adventure—taking the company public.

"Nothing's Going to Change"? Don't Believe It

Years after his close call with a traditional private equity company, Paul Spiegelman did find the right fit for the company he founded, Beryl Health. The incoming CEO of Stericycle, a medical waste disposal company, reached out to Spiegelman. Although Spiegelman had never heard of Stericycle, the CEO had heard about how Spiegelman was championing the power of culture. He wanted to learn how to improve the culture of the company he had taken over.

Stericycle had a very positive entrepreneurial culture, but it focused almost entirely on financial outcomes. Its teams had learned to value customer service, but the company had not yet incorporated the employee as a key stakeholder in the business. The CEO made it clear he was interested in acquiring Beryl Health, but equally interested in learning from its exceptional culture.

Strategic buyers often pose an outsized risk to the smaller company's culture, which the bigger company often consumes. To make matters worse, Stericycle was a public company, and

Spiegelman worried that the imperative to hit the earnings forecast every quarter might overtake the necessity to elevate the culture. But just as a buyer will focus on the future of the company they are acquiring, Spiegelman looked past Stericycle's existing culture and imagined what it might become. One encouraging sign: the CEO was open to change.

"I felt like he was very vulnerable and genuine in sharing that with me and then wanting to learn from me, whether we made a deal or not," says Spiegelman. "So that gave me a lot of confidence that the work we did could rub off on this larger company."

Spiegelman sold Beryl to Stericycle, and it turned out to be a great match. Stericycle incorporated the traditions that were important to Beryl's employees, such as their annual holiday party, and Spiegelman got a new position within the acquiring company: Chief Culture Officer. After 28 years of fostering great culture in a small company, he wanted to see whether he could scale his guiding principles to a large, multinational company.

If there's one thing Spiegelman wishes he had known going into the sale, it's that things really will change, even if the buyer signals that the acquisition will operate as a stand-alone division. After all, Stericycle wasn't really in the same business as Beryl Health, so there was less of a need to fully integrate, and they respected that Beryl had a big platform.

"Part of their message was 'Nothing's going to change, we're just going to leave you alone,' and that was attractive to me. In hindsight they could have been more realistic about the things that would change," says Spiegelman.

REMEMBER:

Don't expect that someone is going to write a $50 million check and then change nothing. Generally, a financial buyer is going to change less than a strategic, but no matter what they tell you, things will not be the same. Hopefully they will be better.

Now on the other side of the transaction, Spiegelman has spent five years in a company that goes through forty or fifty acquisitions a year, and he has seen a tendency to use the line that "nothing will change" to encourage companies to join. Spiegelman is working to modify that approach, by making it more transparent. Now they reassure the acquired company's CEO that they won't come in and start cutting jobs or slashing benefits, but there will be changes, not least because Stericycle is a larger company with far greater resources.

The reality is that things will not be the same from the moment that you sell. For starters, as I learned when we sold Data Return to Divine, there will be a boss. You and your team will also have to connect with new colleagues, suss out unspoken rules, adapt to unfamiliar rituals, and learn new processes. Almost certainly, all of you will have to deal with a different HR department. Assuming that you dug into due diligence and took a deep look inside the acquirer before the transaction closed, you know there's a good chance that many changes will work out and ultimately benefit your company.

However, change of any kind—even positive change—is potentially destabilizing, sometimes unknowable, and often uncomfortable for people. The day after the close, one of your first challenges—assuming that you stay on with the company—will be to engage your team's anxiety over the change that's coming and turn it into confidence.

Leaving the Company? There Are Still Hard Choices

Many an entrepreneur dreams of financial freedom, and when you sell your business, you have a very good chance of achieving it. But with that freedom come problems and feelings not everyone expects.

"It was a lot harder than I thought. I don't know if there's a secret to it. I fully admit it's a high-class problem. I was much richer, but less happy after selling," says Cory Janssen.

Following Investopedia's sale, Janssen had committed to working for his acquirer. However, he quickly realized he wasn't going to stay beyond the transition period. It wasn't that Forbes was a bad fit for his company—although they did introduce a Manhattan dress code to Janssen's casual Edmonton office, to the confusion of many. On the contrary, the Forbes family made quite an impression on Janssen, and he came to admire them. The problem was that after so many years of steering his own ship, Janssen, like many entrepreneurs, was basically unemployable. With the head office thousands of miles away—and with the mounting frustrations of dealing with the management in New York—Janssen soon saw that he wasn't the right man to lead a large organization's division.

Back at home, Janssen's wife, whom he met at university, had her own rewarding career. She loved her work, but after Janssen sold his business, there was no longer any need for her to help support the family. For many others, that new circumstance would just add another option—to quit her job if she preferred not to work—but Janssen and his wife had young children. All of a sudden, keeping her job meant bearing the weight of conflicting emotions. If she opted to continue working, she would be choosing to leave her young children every day—because she wanted to, not because she had to. It was a more emotionally difficult choice than it ever had been.

Janssen had a similarly paralyzing freedom to deal with. Every time he stayed at the office until seven at night, a practice that was just routine while he was building Investopedia, it occurred to him that nothing was keeping him there financially, and he had no real excuse not to be home helping out with his family. After he transitioned out of Forbes, his newfound free time forced him to get to know himself a lot better. He found himself questioning what he actually enjoyed doing, what he actually wanted to build.

Before the sale, he had set personal goals that had to do with net worth. Once he reached them, he tended to add a zero to his numerical North Star and make that new number his next mission. But after his company was acquired, he realized he had accomplished his last money-based goal. It just didn't make a meaningful difference to strive toward ten times the amount hc alrcady had. It was time to figure out what comes next. He didn't have an answer for a long time, and during those months and years he lived with an uncomfortable void where purpose should be.

The answer came from an unlikely place—the problem itself. If Janssen was finding very few resources to help him deal with these questions, then maybe others needed information, too. In fact, there was very little teaching available for entrepreneurs on how to prepare their companies for sale, which was all too obvious to investors—many complained about the dearth of sellers who were realistic about valuations and had their affairs in order. Janssen decided to build a site called Divestopedia, dedicated to exit planning.

"Everyone wants the company doing $10 million in EBITDA that's going to sell right now, but the fact of the matter is there are only so many larger businesses of high quality," says Janssen. "To get great deal flow, the best thing you can do is educate the entrepreneurs."

His advice to CEOs thinking of selling their business is to do what he calls "pre-due diligence:" taking a disciplined approach to every aspect of the business, so that the company is already prepared when the time comes to sell. It took until the middle of his own due diligence before Janssen realized how much of a cowboy he had been about handling his company's documents. Hustling to meet the buyer's requests, he ended up having to add clauses to old contracts, stipulating what would happen when there was a change of control. At the last minute before the sale, he had to scramble even to find the relevant contracts from eight years prior, and then ask employees to sign off on the changes—something he shouldn't have been focusing on at such a pivotal time.

Janssen learned that a great way to avoid those headaches is to look at your business through the eyes of an outside investor from time to time. Adopting an investor's mindset can prevent you from falling into lazy habits on the back end of the business, which will dilute your credibility when the time comes to sell.

In the years since Janssen sold Investopedia, the company has changed hands twice, most recently to InterActiveCorp, which holds such titles as Match.com and About.com. It now receives about twenty million visits a month and employs four times the number of people it did when Janssen sold it to Forbes. Most of the editorial positions have moved to New York, but he is happy to see that between thirty and forty developers still work out of the old office in Edmonton.

"It has survived and thrived long after we left. I'm not involved with it, but it's nice to see that it lives on," he says.

The emotion that comes with an event can be difficult to predict until it happens. You might expect to feel one way about leaving the company you founded, but there is a good chance the actual feeling will surprise you.

Awarding Equity to Employees Is Often Unrewarding

The old trope of "No good deed goes unpunished" describes some of the CEO experience when selling, in that many entrepreneurs act with the best of intentions for their employees and somehow end up with the sense that it was all for nothing. In almost every case, it turns out to be a matter of misdirected efforts based on misunderstandings. Giving equity is, for an entrepreneur, a real honor—a gesture of trust and belonging, and an exciting opportunity to share in the growth their work is helping to build. But not everyone shares this excitement. Don't let it get you down if this happens.

Most people are less comfortable with risk than entrepreneurs. It's the reason they didn't start their own business, betting it all on a dream. Instead, they work for yours and receive a predictable paycheck. Jack Cohen, the commercial real estate financier, routinely gave out 20 to 35 percent of his company's ownership to senior management. He feels he never really got a good return out of awarding a stake in the enterprise they were building. Many of the staff that worked the longest hours and worried the most were not the ones who had ownership. They just chose to have an ownership mentality.

Part of the problem stems from a calculation some people make when they receive equity. After their base salary and bonus, they consider equity to be a form of deferred compensation. When there is a market downturn or something else goes wrong, their valuation of that equity declines. Cohen's senior management seemed to expect their salaries and bonuses should rise in response to that loss, even as Cohen and the company suffered alongside them.

"It was all I could do to not scream bloody murder," remembers Cohen. "I learned that most people want the upside, but they don't want the downside. So, on that basis, pay them cash."

Even when the gift does come in the form of cash, a clear narrative should accompany that gesture, or employees won't necessarily understand what the money is for. Having never gone through the sale of a company they worked for, they may not understand that the CEO is trying to convey deep gratitude and a sense that they are part of a family. Instead, the recipients may just think this is standard operating procedure when a transaction occurs.

Cory Janssen found himself in the same confusing predicament when he went out of his way to do something nice for his employees, following the sale of Investopedia to Forbes. He tried to negotiate with the acquirer a bonus for the employees, but they refused and said the money would have to come out of his own pocket. So he reached deep. To ensure that employees got a fair distribution, he built a little formula that incorporated factors like years of employment and current salary. Almost every employee got a bonus in the tens or hundreds of thousands—a significant outcome, especially when most employees were still in their careers' early stages. The receptionist received at least $10,000, for example, and the more senior people saw a lot more.

"It's not Google money, but I expected them to appreciate it," says Janssen. "Not one person thanked us, and we got multiple people who came back and complained that we'd created a tax problem for them."

It was an embittering episode—in Janssen's mind, a complete waste of money. Today, when Janssen meets with someone hoping to sell their business, he shares what he learned from the experience, which tends to resonate. The takeaway for him was that entrepreneurs quite often follow the Golden Rule when they would be better off modifying it. They try to do for others what they themselves would have appreciated, but for many employees, money that flows through a company is depersonalized.

Just as Jack discovered, you never know until the chips are down who has an ownership mentality over your company and who simply sees it as a job like any other. For Janssen's employees, changing ownership was less of a big deal than he expected. They wanted to know about their vacation time and their pay, and once that had been established, their heads were back in the work.

Post Merger: The Consequences of Miscalculating Culture

"I sit around and ask myself, what could I have done differently . . . What *should* I have done differently?" says Richard Ellis. "Every day I feel guilty about the outcome for my employees, but I was able to check the box on financial freedom. I lead a super comfortable life, so it's hard to complain a lot."

Ellis is not alone in having mixed feelings about the sale of his company. Some CEOs describe the sense of loss as akin to the death of a close family member, and the simultaneous thrill of financial and professional freedom as akin to the birth of a child. It's a confusing combination, but Ellis' story is particularly instructive because he has been able to work through the turbulence and come out the other side stronger.

In 1999, Ellis took over the family business, Musslewhite Trucking, part of the West Texas oil and gas field services industry. His business had less than a million dollars in revenue that year, a benchmark he would often look back on in the coming years.

During the thirteen years he owned the company, it went through dramatic ups and downs that shaped Ellis' mindset. The big picture was of rapid growth and transformation several times over, but a close-up look would show that he had it all on the line, day after day. The energy service industry is highly cyclical at the best of times, but in 2009, when oil prices dropped from $140 to $25 a barrel—coupled with the Great Recession— Ellis had to take on a significant debt load, and he had to personally guarantee every cent.

"We came out of it, but it was scary, so I think those life experiences have made me super cautious," says Ellis.

After a positive cash flow, negative earnings year in that downturn, the company made a rapid recovery and saw significant growth in 2011. By 2012, the company was home to 650 employees, with revenue of $180 million (up from less than one million a decade earlier), and EBITDA of about $70 million.

Having paid down the debt, Ellis saw two options ahead: lever up to try to move the needle again, or value the company for sale and take some chips off the table. He was very much off the heels of 2009 and the fear that year had evoked. The thought of borrowing a lot of money again, only to find himself in another down cycle, was just too much. Ellis decided to sell, largely because the hits he had taken had changed his fun-to-fear ratio, with the fear looming far larger than the fun. Fear could only be put aside with risk taken off the table. He started a process and found a buyer.

The sale was a hybrid, with some elements of a financial acquisition and others of a strategic. Although Globe Energy purchased Ellis' company, a private equity firm, which made most of the financial decisions, controlled its board. During due diligence, when Ellis sat across the table from the private equity sponsors and the management of the acquiring company, he saw them as a united force. After the transaction, he would realize that the two sides were really separate factions, with different interests and different approaches to business.

Ellis and the other leaders of the newly merged company were all aligned around the over-arching goal—dramatic growth—but the financial team at the private equity firm seemed more focused on sophisticated financial engineering, using leverage to find ways outside of the company's operations to create wealth. The management team was happy to receive the money from this debt load, but they didn't have a solid plan to pay it back. The amount of risk the company was taking on floored Ellis, even as everyone around him seemed comfortable with it. Based on past experience, he knew that a massive debt-to-equity ratio in a super cyclical business was a disaster waiting to happen.

The difference in approach extended to his acquirer's spendthrift culture, which in comparison with Ellis' company looked like a riot of free lunches, flashy vehicles, and unchecked expense accounts. The company had a hunting lease and endless entertainment options. In Ellis' company, you only spent money if you had to. Where a stripped-down pickup would do, the new company bought King Ranch pickups and super-stylish uniforms.

"Honestly, I didn't do my diligence to determine what the cultural differences were, and that was one of my biggest mistakes. I was a true believer, and I preached from the mountaintop, this is going to be great!" says Ellis.

During due diligence, he thought the similarities between the two companies would mean that the cultural mix would automatically go well. He also thought the transition would be a boon for his employees. Unusually for a sale with strategic elements, everyone down to the rank and file would keep their jobs, their compensation level, and their seniority. The top management team received a significant bonus, and two or three layers of management down also saw a modest bonus. In theory, the staff would have more opportunities in a larger company and more ways to move around the organization.

The reality was more complicated. Even though some of his management team were placed in positions with lofty titles in the new company—his CFO became the Chief Accounting

Officer, for example—the chain of command proved flexible, and their authority felt like an illusion. In the acquirer's culture, if you didn't like the answer from your structural supervisor, you just went straight to the CEO, who would contradict his senior management team and give the employee the answer they wanted. For Ellis' management team, it was a rude awakening. Their approach had been to hire the right people, train them with all the right tools, and then get out of their way. Any attempt to resolve things outside of the chain of command had been decisively discouraged.

"I felt really sad for my employees, because they no longer had the ability to lead. They really felt demoralized, and we lost so many of them. I felt I betrayed all of my employees," Ellis says.

All of the management team is gone now, and hundreds of others also left. Only a few equipment operators and dispatchers remain. Perhaps the problem lay in the clannish culture of a company created in a small town, where there is a fair amount of nepotism and insularity, and that us-versus-them mentality affected the team in more fundamental ways. Even now, the acquirer's original employees have higher social standing, and everyone is keenly aware of who bought who. The handful of people who transitioned to the acquirer and remain still have to work every day just to prove they belong in the group.

Looking back, Ellis has a theory about what he could have done to ease his team members' transition. If he had left right away, instead of remaining for half of his three-year transition plan, his colleagues would not have had the false sense of comfort that comes with having their previous leadership in place. If it's clear that people need to engrain themselves in a new culture with a new brand on their shirt, they can often handle it. The former leaders' continued presence represents a hope that things might return to the old ways, and that false sense of security can impede their adjustment.

However, in the weeks following the sale, Ellis was more concerned about the company's high leverage. He was torn: his instincts told him they were taking on too much debt financing, but the private equity guys were really smart and presumably knew what they were doing. They had a sophisticated understanding of their financial instruments, they had all attended Harvard or Columbia, they lived in Manhattan and worked under the direction of a billionaire—these were world-class players. They owned businesses ranging from a crane company to Ford Models, but energy was hot at the time, so they brought that into their portfolio, too.

They were missing some key experience, though, because their whole careers were rooted in finance. Straight out of college, they had jumped into analyst positions and worked their way up to managing directors. None of them had ever made payroll or led a company. It's not enough to master financial instruments if you are clueless about what it actually takes to earn the money with which to pay off those instruments. The lack of hands-on experience takes even more of a toll in the industrial world, where understanding working people's mindsets is critical.

"I think a lack of any blue-collar experience or even any

ability to empathize with the blue-collar lifestyle really hurts them," says Ellis. His own strength lay in his ability to go "between the boardroom and the backhoe" with equal comfort.

Unfortunately, Ellis ignored the gathering dangers as much as he could, largely because the equity team seemed confident the money would materialize. Not only had the private equity firm written Ellis an enormous check, but he had a lot of equity rolled over into the new company, and it was the job of the financial team to know a good bet when they saw one. He stood to make a whole lot more.

When the company decided to make some more acquisitions, they put out a cash call, and Ellis wrote another big check into the company. He had even more on the line when the leverage finally caught up to the business, and it fell into the hands of the creditors. Too late, Ellis' reservations were vindicated. He was completely locked out and lost all his remaining equity.

Post Exit: Building a New Identity

In the months and years after the decline and fall of Global Energy Services, Ellis came to question not only his decisions around the transaction but also the role of work in his life.

"I was super driven by trying to make money, to the extent that I ignored my family. I've got nine and eleven-year-old little boys, and before this, I was nonexistent in their lives," says Ellis.

Even though his company failed, he still attained all of his money-related goals. In the aftermath, he re-examined what made him sacrifice so much for that money—and why he still felt so lost. To find support, he turned to his community of fellow entrepreneurs. In 2011, Ellis had taken the Stagen leadership course in Dallas, which offered him a number of tools, including a personal coach.

For a few weeks, he worked with that coach to explore the roots of his depression and build an idea of what his next stage of life would look like. He discovered that he was dealing, in part, with a loss of identity. The CEO role had made his sense of self one and the same with his company, and it felt really good—being the boss came with a lot of respect and credibility.

"Everybody was like, 'Oh my gosh, there he is!' There was this sense of ego that came with it that I didn't realize I had at the time," says Ellis.

If he were no longer the boss, who was he? He shared his thoughts with peers in Young Presidents Organization (YPO). One of his forum mates there took him aside and suggested they think it through together. He had seen Ellis struggling in 2009 with the sudden downturn of his business, and he asked why he seemed just as depressed, now that he was sitting on a pile of money. It was hard to admit that he had a real problem, that his ego was wrapped up in his business—that had he understood and acknowledged that fact earlier, he might have made better decisions when selling the company.

To the younger Ellis, the meaning of life had been to get up every day and go to work really early, then stay really late. It was going to take some doing to shed his Captain of Industry persona and convert it into a passion for everything life had to offer outside of the office, starting with his family. What he discovered was that life could be much more broad and diverse than when work was his only focal point. He traveled extensively with his wife and explored the world in a way he had never allowed time for before.

His new life was fulfilling, and it gradually grew clear that his purpose on this planet was not to be a water logistician or even a businessman. His purpose was to raise a family and to engage in business only when he wanted.

Careful not to fall into the workaholic trap from his previous career, he started a small private equity fund to keep himself mentally stimulated, investing in a handful of companies—transportation, web development, a finance company, and a hamburger joint. He spends half of the work week at the office, advising these management teams and helping to grow the companies, but he does it for the fun of it and thereby eludes the vice-grip of ambition.

Still, one question haunted him, and it wasn't really a question he was asking himself, but one that everyone else seemed to ask. When he showed up at the soccer field to watch his sons practice, other parents would inevitably ask what he did for a living. He didn't feel secure enough to say, "You're looking at it. This is what I do." He knew the world looked at him differently, now that he wasn't leading a company. At age 45, he can't yet pull off the role of a retiree or even a semi-retired person, investing his money after a long career. For the first three years after the sale, he would hem and haw and tell them he didn't really know and couldn't exactly explain.

"People look at you with this blank stare, like, 'okay loser, go get a job,'" says Ellis. But with time, he gained the confidence to look them in the eye and say, "I'm a father, I'm a husband, I'm a professional when I want to be, and I'm a world explorer."

"Put that in your suck-it bucket!" he adds, presumably silently. "It's fantastic. Couldn't be happier. I can't be any luckier, really."

Now It's Your Turn

Over the course of this book, we've looked at the despair that comes from selling to the wrong guys and the joy of selling to the right guys. We've seen the pain that follows a bad investor and the uplifting effect of a great investor. We've talked about how preparing for a sale starts with preparing yourself. We've taken a deep dive into the reasons for selling and identified all the options. We've mapped out the path to selling consciously, where there is a good outcome for every stakeholder, beyond the seller and the acquirer. We've thought through the process for identifying the right buyer and unpacked hard-won insights for selling smart. And we've dug into the challenges that come after the sale.

Now it's your turn. This is your opportunity to take what resonates and apply it to your own unique circumstances, as you begin the process of selling the enterprise that you've spent a good part of your life creating. As you take that step, recall what I said at the book's outset: it's possible to sell your business, get rich, and fail at the same time. (In fact, in many cases it's *probable.*) What I wish for you is the courage and judgment to take the path less traveled: to sell without selling out.

The pivotal moment in an entrepreneur's life is not the first check you frame on your wall, and it's not the triumph of proving everyone wrong and succeeding. It's the choice you make when you pass that ownership into new hands that can take the business forward into its next life, with or without you.

This is why we started Satori, so that entrepreneurs don't have to make an impossible choice among bad outcomes. We set out to create a firm that forms a real partnership with an entrepreneur and provides the capital and the expertise to help their business become the best version of itself. It really is possible to leave your legacy intact and sell to those who share your idea of what is important. It's possible to look back years later and say to yourself, "I made a great choice." You don't have to be a hero to ensure that outcome. You just have to take a stand.

ACKNOWLEDGMENTS

This book would not exist without the help and support of a great many people, and I'm glad to have the opportunity to offer my thanks to them here.

Thank you to the team that actually brought this book into being: Jessa Gamble, for skillful writing and the ability to capture my voice; Bill Breen, for insightful editing; Hope Kahan and Keera Ketterman, for tireless project management; Clint Greenleaf, for invaluable advice and guidance; Pete Garceau and Sheila Parr, for graceful design; and Danyelle De Jong and Ellen Henderson, for special assistance along the way. You all helped me create an extraordinary outcome for this project that exceeded anything I could have hoped for.

My deep gratitude goes to the business leaders who agreed to share their stories and insights in this book: Jack Cohen, Richard Ellis, Kevin Fallon, Jane Greyf, Cory Janssen, Mike McGill, Gary Moon, Shawn Nelson, John Ofenloch, Britt Peterson, Clint Scott, Paul Spiegelman, John Squires, Fred Thiel, Garry Waldrum, and Scott Winicour. It would have been easy to share only the "edited for TV" versions of your stories, but you gave us your real, heartfelt experiences, and in doing so, you provided a genuine service to the leaders who will follow the path behind you.

To my partners and the team at Satori Capital: You all carried an extra share of the load to give me the time and space to devote to this project, and your support means the world to me. Thank you for always serving as an inspiring example of what the principles of conscious capitalism look like in action.

I could not have written this book without my experiences at Data Return and the team that went on that journey with me. Between our rocket-fueled growth, the IPO, the dot-com crash, the sale that wasn't, selling to the wrong guys, and doing it over again the right way, we had one thrill ride of a decade. It wasn't easy, but you stuck with me as we learned things the hard way, and you never stopped believing in what we were building together. It is my hope that what we learned back then will help others now through this book. Thank you for everything.

Thank you to the team at Conscious Capitalism, Inc., and Conscious Capitalism Press, particularly Alexander McCobin and Corey Blake, and to my fellow members of the Conscious Capitalism board of directors. Thanks go as well to my colleagues at YPO, particularly the North Texas chapter and the members of YPO's Entrepreneurship and Innovation Network. Special thanks go to Jody Grant for his mentorship over many years.

I am also very grateful to the CEOs and leaders who made time in their busy schedules to read early copies of this book.

Your enthusiastic comments served as our first concrete evidence that we had succeeded in creating something useful and meaningful, and your support is truly appreciated.

I could not write any list of acknowledgments without including a thank-you to my wife, Tisha, who has been by my side through every momentous occasion, extraordinary experience, and tough decision described in this book, along with several that aren't as printable. For every new and out-there adventure I've dreamed up, she's been right there with me, adding her insight and cheering me on, and I could not have done it all without her support.

Finally, I want to thank all the people who have provided good counsel, insightful feedback, and strategic guidance to me at various critical moments in the last couple of decades. Your wisdom was offered without expectation and in the spirit of genuine service, and this book, which I wrote with all your lessons in mind, is my attempt to pay that forward on a large scale.

ELEVATE HUMANITY THROUGH BUSINESS.

WE BELIEVE THAT BUSINESS IS GOOD BECAUSE IT CREATES VALUE, IT IS ETHICAL BECAUSE IT IS BASED ON VOLUNTARY EXCHANGE, IT IS NOBLE BECAUSE IT CAN ELEVATE OUR EXISTENCE, AND IT IS HEROIC BECAUSE IT LIFTS PEOPLE OUT OF POVERTY AND CREATES PROSPERITY. FREE ENTERPRISE CAPITALISM IS THE MOST POWERFUL SYSTEM FOR SOCIAL COOPERATION AND HUMAN PROGRESS EVER CONCEIVED. IT IS ONE OF THE MOST COMPELLING IDEAS WE HUMANS HAVE EVER HAD. BUT WE CAN ASPIRE TO EVEN MORE.

Excerpt from the Conscious Capitalist Credo. Read it in its entirety at www.consciouscapitalism.org/about/credo.

Conscious Capitalism is a paradigm that places people at the center of business. Conscious Capitalism, Inc. is an organization that brings businesses and business leaders on a conscious journey to elevate humanity through business by convening conscious capitalists, providing learning and development opportunities, and garnering PR for businesses, making the world a better place.

There are Conscious Capitalism events happening around the globe each week with over eighty conscious capitalist communities in twenty countries whose purpose is to connect with others, provide inspiration through storytelling, and give information and resources that allow community members to become stronger voices for business as a force for good.

We invite you, either as an individual or as a business, to get involved by joining us at a Conscious Capitalism event or a learning and development offering, and by sharing your story.

Learn more and join the movement at www.consciouscapitalism.org.